S0-EKM-590

THE PATH OF OUR GROWTH IN LIFE

WITNESS LEE

Living Stream Ministry
Anaheim, California

© 2001 Living Stream Ministry

All rights reserved. No part of this work may be reproduced or transmitted in any form or by any means—graphic, electronic, or mechanical, including photocopying, recording, or information storage and retrieval systems—without written permission from the publisher.

First Edition, November 2001.

ISBN 0-7363-1470-9

Published by

Living Stream Ministry
2431 W. La Palma Ave., Anaheim, CA 92801 U.S.A.
P. O. Box 2121, Anaheim, CA 92814 U.S.A.

Printed in the United States of America

01 02 03 04 05 06 07 / 10 9 8 7 6 5 4 3 2 1

CONTENTS

PREFACE

This book is a collection of messages given by Brother Witness Lee in Taipei in 1951. It contains nine messages that lead the saints along the path of the growth in life that they may enter into the identification with Christ's death and resurrection, see how human opinion is versus the resurrection power of God, and live and serve by revelation.

CHAPTER ONE

THE PATH OF OUR GROWTH IN LIFE

If someone desires to look into the Christian life, he must realize that the Christian life is basically a matter of life. All other matters, such as reading the Bible, preaching the gospel, and serving, are also wrapped up with life. Once this matter of life has been dealt with, all other matters are resolved. Life is the origin and foundation of everything. It is our way, our power, and our light. Life is everything to us. Since life is such a crucial matter, our most urgent need is to learn how to touch the way of life so that we may grow in life. Hence, the following items are the most important matters concerning the way of life.

RECEIVING THE LORD'S LIFE BY CALLING ON THE LORD

First of all, every brother and sister should have a clear understanding that at the time they prayed and called on the Lord, the Lord's life entered into them. This is not a doctrine but a reality. When a person calls on the Lord, the Lord's life will enter into him.

LIVING IN THE LORD'S LIFE

Second, God's intention is not only that a person would receive the life of the Lord, but that after a person is saved, he also would live in such a life in an absolute way. It is not God's intention that man would go to a heavenly mansion or to the heavens after he has received God's life; rather, God wants man to live in such a life.

LIVING IN THE LORD'S LIFE BY LOVING THE LORD

Third, what should man do to live in God's life since it is God's desire for us to do so? The essential, indispensable thing to do is to love the Lord. Even though all the saved ones have received the Lord's life, those who do not love the Lord will not live in His life. The more a person loves the Lord, the more he will live in the Lord's life. If a person does not love the Lord, he will not be able to live in the Lord's life. John 15 says that the Lord is the vine and that we are the branches. It also says that we have to abide in Him. John chapters fifteen and sixteen speak about abiding (15:4-7) on the one hand, and about loving the Lord (16:27) on the other hand. Only when we love the Lord will we allow Him to abide in us. The degree to which we love the Lord determines the degree to which we will live by His life.

The epistle that the Lord wrote to the messenger of the church in Ephesus in Revelation 2 says that the Lord had one thing against the church in Ephesus—she had left her first love (v. 4). She was irreproachable in her works, but she was short of love. Eventually the Lord said that unless she repented, He would remove her lampstand out of its place (v. 5). As a result, she would not be given to partake of the fruit of the tree of life (v. 7). The lampstand is a matter of light, and the tree of life is something related to life. Every time we leave our love for the Lord, we lose light and life. If a brother in the church in Ephesus had risen up to love the Lord in order to gain the Lord's life, he would have received the light of life to maintain the testimony of life. Once we leave our love for the Lord, we lose life and light. We are here not to preach a doctrine to people but to guide them to the path of life. Doctrine cannot enable people to live in the Lord's life. Only walking on the path of life can help people to live in the Lord's life.

Everyone who wants to live in the Lord's life has to love the Lord. This love is not a love of adoration but a love of romance like the love that is spoken of in the Song of Songs. Without such a love, we will have nothing to do with the path of life. For us to live in the Lord's life, we have to love the Lord and even be deeply in love with Him. Our love for the

Lord enables us to receive His life and light. If we find that we do not love the Lord, we have to pray, "Lord, up to this moment I still do not love You. Although I know that I have Your life, I do not have any love for You. I do adore You, but I do not love You. I cannot sense Your freshness, Your beauty, and Your loveliness. O Lord, save me and grant me Your love."

No one can serve the Lord without loving Him. Madame Guyon's most precious trait was that she loved the Lord. If you want to live in the life and nature of another person, you have to live in love. Then that person's nature will become your nature because you love him, and your nature will become his nature because that person loves you. The two natures not only interact, but they also are interchanged. It is the same with us in regard to the Lord. If we want to live in the life and nature of the Lord, we have to love Him. I can show you the way and the principle, but I am not able to fill up your lack. You must go and pray by yourself. If we do not love the Lord, there is no way for us to grow in life. When we were saved, we received the Lord's life, but if we do not love the Lord, desire the Lord, and pursue the Lord, then in the end we will at most be like an elderly child. We will be able to pray, read the Bible, and meet with the saints, but we will have no way to live in the Lord's life. The principle here is that only those who love the Lord can live in His life.

LAYING DOWN OUR OPINIONS

Fourth, everyone who lives in the Lord's life not only needs to love the Lord but also should learn to deny himself in an absolute way. In the Gospels there are two groups of people who followed the Lord. One group was composed of brothers, including Peter, John, and James; the other group was composed of sisters, such as Mary and Martha. The brothers followed the Lord, but they did not love the Lord. Consider, for example, the case of Judas. Wherever the Lord went, Judas followed, yet in the end he betrayed the Lord. What about Peter? Can we say that he loved the Lord? We cannot say that he did. Hence, the Lord asked Peter, "Do you love Me?" The Lord asked him several times, to the extent that Peter was puzzled. If he did not love the Lord, then why had he been following the Lord for three and a half years? But he could not say that he did love the Lord, because it did not seem to be the case. Therefore, Peter could only say, "Yes, Lord, You know..." (John 21:15-17). It was the same with John. We also cannot tell for sure that he loved the Lord. In the Gospels it is difficult to find any examples that clearly show us that any of the brothers loved the Lord. This reveals that the brothers represent those who pursue and follow the Lord without loving the Lord.

In the beginning of the New Testament, although there was a group of brothers who followed the Lord without loving Him, there was a group of sisters who knew nothing but to truly love the Lord. These sisters represent those who love the Lord. Thus, the brothers represent those who have a clear mind, and the sisters represent those who are rich in their emotion but are not clear in their mind. However, those who love the Lord are also divided into two categories—Mary represents one category, and Martha represents the other. Both Mary and Martha loved the Lord, but there was a big difference between Mary's love toward the Lord and Martha's love toward the Lord. Mary was one who put her opinions aside whereas Martha was one who expressed all her opinions.

The subject of John 11 ought to be "The opinions of man in opposition to the power of resurrection." In John 11 God's intention was to express the power of the Lord's resurrection through Lazarus. However, this expression of the power of life was frustrated by human opinions. Lazarus was sick, and God in His sovereignty intended for Lazarus to be sick unto death; however, Martha and Mary sent people to ask the Lord to come and heal him. The Lord did not go right away; instead, He stayed where He was until Lazarus was dead. Before the death of Lazarus, the disciples of the Lord urged Him to go to Lazarus, but the Lord did not go. After Lazarus died, the Lord wanted to go to Lazarus, but the disciples did not agree, saying that the Jews might stone Him. Then the Lord told them that Lazarus had fallen asleep and that He had to go to wake him out of his sleep. Yet the disciples were still there expressing their opinions as a frustration to the Lord. When the Lord Jesus arrived at the place where Lazarus was, Martha went to meet Him and immediately expressed her opinion, saying, "If You had been here, my brother would not have died" (v. 21). What she really meant was that the Lord should have come before Lazarus was dead, but now that he was dead and buried there was no need for the Lord to have come. Then the Lord told her, "Your brother will rise again" (v. 23). But Martha said, "I know that he will rise again in the resurrection in the last day" (v. 24). While she thought she knew what resurrection was, she was actually speaking her own opinion, expounding the Lord's word in a way that would postpone the present resurrection to the last day. Then the Lord said to her, "I am the resurrection and the life; he who believes into Me, even if he should die, shall live....Do you believe this?" (vv. 25-26). Martha immediately replied, "Yes, Lord; I have believed that You are the Christ, the Son of God" (v. 27). The Lord was speaking about the east, but Martha was speaking about the west; the Lord was speaking about the heavens, but Martha was speaking about the earth. Martha seemed to answer different questions than the ones she was asked.

Moreover, after Martha had spoken this way, she went to call Mary and told her that the Lord was calling her. This must also have been Martha's opinion because we cannot find anywhere that the Lord had said this. When Mary went to see the Lord, she expressed the same opinion as Martha had. Then the Lord wept (v. 35). Many people think that the Lord wept because He was sad, but the real reason that the Lord wept was because He realized that even Mary did not know Him. After this the Lord asked the people to take away the stone that lay before Lazarus' tomb, and Martha, who was used to answering questions that no one had asked her, expressed her opinion again, saying, "By now he smells" (v. 39). This whole story is full of human opinions. Opinions hinder the move of the Lord. Thus, a person who lives in the Lord's life must be one who puts his opinion aside. Opinions are the greatest enemy and hindrance to the expression of the life of God through us. Hence, we must have love and no opinions.

FOLLOWING THE SENSE OF LIFE

Fifth, when we love the Lord and put aside our opinions, we will be full of the Lord's feeling. Then we will have to follow the Lord and walk according to the sense of life in our spirit. When love comes in and our opinions go out, the sense of life will be activated. Then we can live and walk according to such a sense. Many times within us we do not have much spiritual sensation because we have too many opinions and not very much love. The secret of receiving the sense of life is to love much and not have any opinions. When we love the Lord absolutely and do not have any opinions, surely we will have more of the sense of life.

Throughout the entire Scriptures we see that Mary expressed her opinion only once, while Peter expressed his opinion on many different occasions. Although this always got Peter into trouble, he still had opinions. In Matthew 16 the Lord told His disciples that He had to go to Jerusalem, suffer many things, and be killed. After hearing this Peter quickly said, "This shall by no means happen to You!" (v. 22). The Lord then immediately turned and said to him, "Get behind Me, Satan!" (v. 23). This shows us that Peter's opinion was Satan himself; Satan was hiding in Peter's opinion. Then the Lord continued, "You are not setting your mind on the things of God, but on the things of men....If anyone wants to come after Me, let him deny himself" (vv. 23-24). The Lord first spoke of Satan, then of the mind set on the things of men, and then of denying the self. This indicates that Satan is expressed through the human mind with its opinions and that our opinions should be rejected.

Later the Lord Jesus brought Peter, James, and John up to a high mountain and was transfigured before them. Suddenly, Moses and Elijah appeared to them. When Peter saw this, he immediately expressed his opinion again. God eventually had to interrupt him (17:1-5). Later, when they came to Capernaum, those who collected the temple tax came to Peter and said, "Does not your Teacher pay the temple tax?" Peter expressed his opinion right away and said, "Yes." After this, when Peter came into the house and before he opened his mouth, the Lord asked him, "What do you think, Simon? From whom do the kings of the earth receive custom or poll tax, from their sons or from strangers?" (vv. 24-25). What the Lord meant when He asked this was, Why did you say that I have to pay the poll tax for making repairs in the temple of God when you just heard on the mountain that I am the Son of God? In the end the Lord told Peter to go fishing and to take the stater from the mouth of the first fish that he would catch and use that to pay the tax (v. 27). I believe that Peter must have learned a big lesson while he was fishing. The Lord had told him to cast a hook, but he must have wondered where he could find a fish in such a boundless sea? Even if the fish came, would it actually have a stater in its mouth? In this difficult situation Peter learned a big lesson.

Now we come to Mary. She expressed her opinion only one time. By the time she anointed the Lord, she did not have any more words or opinions. The voices, opinions, and judgments of the disciples are evident in their following of the Lord, but we cannot hear the voice or opinion of Mary. She did not have any opinion, and thus she was full of feeling within. Although others did not sense that the Lord was going to die, she sensed it. When others did not know that they needed to anoint the Lord, she sensed that she had to anoint the Lord. Have you seen this? When we love much and have little opinion, we will be rich in our inner feeling. Many times we have little feeling because we have a lot of opinion and not much love. When we have much opinion, we will not have much feeling. Then once we do have some inner feeling, we should live according to it.

NOT BEING INFLUENCED
BY THINGS THAT ARE GOOD OR RIGHT

Sixth, we should never be influenced by what is good or by what is right. Many times as Christians we are easily influenced by things that are good or by things that are right, yet this should not be the case. For example, when we see a humble brother, we may want to imitate him. This is not wrong, but we who follow the Lord should not be influenced by other people. Instead, we should be directed by the inner sense of life. We may use another example. There was once a sister who was very zealous for the preaching of the gospel. When the young brothers and sisters saw her, they all tried to imitate her. Eventually they did not care for anything other than the preaching of the gospel. In the fellowship meeting they would rise up and rebuke those who did not preach the gospel. When some other young sisters heard their speaking, they also were stirred up to be zealous for the gospel. Do you think this is good? This is a way most welcomed by Christianity today, but this is not the way that God wants us to take. It is not a matter of whether something is good or bad; what matters is the way that we take. This sister's way was a way of promoting and urging, not one of life. It was a way in which people were influenced by outward things, not by the inner life.

When we lay down our opinions, we will have an inner sense, and when we follow and are led by this sense to preach the gospel, then our gospel preaching will be something that comes from within. This is the way of life. If we are those who are influenced by outward things, it will be absolutely impossible for us to live in the Lord's life. Consider our former example. Is that kind of service a service of the spirit or a service of the soul? No doubt, it is a service of the soul. Although the service itself is good, its source is not proper. This is not a question of good or bad, right or wrong, but a question of the source. As long as we love Him, give our heart to Him, and present ourselves to Him, we will be full of feeling within. Once we have some feeling, we should walk according to it. This is the way of life.

Although we have not mentioned the cross, in the way of life there is the cross. Although we have not mentioned the power of resurrection, the way of life is full of the resurrection life. Human opinion is the expression of the self. When we lay down our opinion, we experience the cross. The most prominent expression of the self is human opinion. Matthew 16 first mentions human opinion, then the self. When the self within us is expressed, it is opinion. Opinion is eventually broken by the cross. When due to our love for the Lord we are willing to lay down our opinion, this is the breaking of the cross. If someone can come to the church in our locality twenty times without seeing us express our opinion, then we are almost matured. Today in serving the Lord, on the positive side, we do not love the Lord enough, but on the negative side, we have too much opinion. This indicates that we have not allowed the cross to do a deep work in us. If we allow the cross to work in us in a deeper way, all our opinions will disappear. Opinion represents the self, and the self is the soul. The work of the cross is to put the soul aside. Living according to the sense of life is actually to live according to the power of resurrection. We should not be influenced by people outwardly or live according to morality or religion; rather, we should live according to the inner sense of life. We should love the Lord, follow the Lord, lay down our opinions absolutely, and live according to the sense of life. This is to live in the Lord's life.

QUESTIONS AND ANSWERS

Question: In my daily life, sometimes I have a word that operates in my heart at a certain time, then after some time there is another word that operates in my heart. Is this the sense of life?

Answer: This is not the sense of life but the teaching of the word. The sense of life is not a teaching that we have heard but our inner feeling. An outward teaching may remind us of our inner feeling, but it is not the sense of life. The genuine sense of life is this: We do not think about denying the self, but because of our love for the Lord, there is a feeling within us when we are loving Him that causes us to deny the self. When we do a certain thing owing to our love for the Lord, this is the sense of life. Even the feeling that we get as a result of others' speaking stems eighty percent from religion and teaching, not from revelation or life.

Suppose someone swings his hand toward your eyes. If this happens, you will automatically close your eyelids. Such a reaction is of life. Suppose, however, that someone told you that your pupils are precious, that your eyelids should protect your pupils, and that when someone swings their hand toward your eyes, you should close your eyelids. In response, you decide that later when someone tries to hit you, you will close your eyelids. This would be something related to teaching and religion. If something is the issue of life and revelation, we do not have to have the understanding concerning it. We do not need an eye doctor's explanation, because we spontaneously close our eyelids when someone tries to hit our eyes.

The Christian life, which has its source in revelation, is actually the Lord Himself. Once we touch Him, we will live and be full of life. Whatever requires the help or the teaching of doctrines is something religious. Although sometimes the word that operates in us may also come from the sense of life, this is usually not the case. For example, when a person says that the word about the Lord's eyes being like a flame of fire is working in his being, I believe that this is eighty percent something religious. The word entering into his heart and working in his being may be the result of his decision, not of the Spirit. Even if it is of the Spirit, it would be at the most only twenty percent.

Anything that requires outward teaching and reminding is not the product of revelation or life. Why do we avoid watching movies? Is it because the Word says that we should not watch movies? Is it because we are afraid that we would not know what to do if the Lord were to come back while we were watching a movie? If the reason we do not watch movies is because of such a fear, then this is something religious. Some people say that if we tell lies, then after we die, we will be judged and our tongue will be cut out. This is a degraded religious thought. However, even such a thought has come into Christianity. When we no longer need the outward reminding of other people, yet we still have the feeling that we should not watch movies, then this is most likely something produced by life. When we love the Lord, draw near to Him, and put aside our opinions, the Lord will have the ground to operate and move freely within us. His operation and His move come from life and will produce a certain sense within us. Once such a feeling comes forth, the Lord comes forth. At this time, regardless of what kind of opinion or thought we may have, we will be willing to lay it down and closely follow the Lord. This is the experience of the cross and of resurrection life.

Question: What is the difference between our natural goodness and the goodness that issues from life?

Answer: In the Bible, there are good people and bad people. Some people are good while some are not good. There are two kinds of goodness, as seen in the stories of Esau versus Jacob, and David versus Saul. Esau was an ethical man whereas Jacob was a crafty person. Esau never deceived anyone and, in terms of ethics, he was a virtuous man. On the contrary Jacob was always a supplanter and a base person. In the story of David and Saul, Saul wanted to kill David, but when David was given the opportunity to kill Saul, he did not kill him. The generosity of David was a kind of goodness. However, Esau's goodness and David's goodness were different. The goodness of Esau came out of his own effort, but the goodness of David was the issue of the power of God.

By nature, many Christians may be like Jacob—loving to supplant—while many unbelievers may be generous. From such a perspective, many Christians seem to be inferior to unbelievers according to nature. Take the case of Jacob, who was crafty from the time he was young. Jacob cheated his brother, his father, his uncle, and his wives. The name *Jacob* can mean "crafty" and "struggler." Although he was such a person, the Bible tells us that Jacob was the one that God loved (Rom. 9:13). From a human perspective, Jacob was far from being a good person. Nevertheless, he was dealt with by God to the point that when he reached old age, God changed his name to *Israel* (Gen. 32:28). Moreover, when he blessed Joseph while he was dying, he genuinely and boldly said that God was the One who had shepherded him all his life (48:15). At that point he did not have any tricks; he simply bowed himself, leaning on the head of his bed (47:31). When he spoke, he spoke for God. Jacob's maturity in his old age was the work of God and was altogether different from Esau's natural nobility. This is the difference between natural goodness and goodness that issues from life.

On the other hand, although David was one who lived before God and had fellowship with God, when God's hand departed from him, he committed a sin (2 Sam. 11). When David's goodness was not sustained by the power of God's life, it did not last. When a person is apart from God, he is evil and filthy. Only when he is living before God is he a noble and upright person, having the genuine goodness of life.

Question: Sometimes I cannot tell if a feeling comes from life or from my mind. How can I discern between the two?

Answer: If we love the Lord and put ourselves aside, we do not need to analyze our feelings; rather, we should simply follow the feeling we receive until we lose the sense of peace.

First of all, as Christians we are like a woman who is married to the Lord (2 Cor. 11:2). The motivation for us to live such a life is that we are married to the Lord and we love Him. Hence, we have to tell the Lord all the time, "Lord, I do this because I love You." Second, we also need to put our opinions aside. When we do this, a sense will rise up within us. Then we have to walk according to this sense. Once we do not have the peace within, we should stop. When a Christian lives by the sense of life, it is not easy for him to feel it. When he makes a mistake, however, he will lose his peace and then he will have some feeling. Therefore, we should simply follow our inner sense and not analyze too much. We may not see the result right away, but when we look back after some years, we will be able to tell that we have made some progress. Thus, it is enough just to love the Lord, lay aside our opinions, and follow the inner sense. We do not need to analyze so many other matters.

Question: Is it a problem if our will is not strong?

Answer: A will that is not strong is a problem. Some people have a strong will by birth, but this natural strength has to be broken. On the other hand, those who are not born with a strong will should ask God to strengthen their will. A will that is not strong is really a problem related to life. When life directs us from within and we follow the leading of life, gradually there will be a strengthening of our will. Our will is not strong because our spirit is not strong enough. If we allow the Lord's life to have the ground in us, our spirit will surely be strong. Once our spirit is strengthened, our soul will be normal, and we will be delivered from all abnormal situations. Some people naturally do not have a smart mind, but because they love the Lord and are strengthened in spirit, they become clear in their mind. Some people were weak in their will, but because of their love for the Lord, their spirit became strong and their will was also strengthened. Hence, if our will is weak, we should pray.

Question: Is the word of God meant to teach us?

Answer: The word of God given to us seems to have at least two sides. On the one hand, the word of God is for our teaching; on the other hand, the word of God is really a book of revelation. It is true that we may read the Bible to receive teaching and golden verses, but more often we should read the Bible in order to receive revelation and enlightenment. When the word of God touches our spirit and gives us a sense in our spirit, this is revelation. Sometimes we take the word of God for our understanding and for us to have a clear mind. This is to take the word as teaching and is religious. In brief, this teaching is something of religion and of the mind, but revelation is something of life and of an inner consciousness.

CHAPTER TWO

READING THE BIBLE

After a Christian is saved, the very first thing he needs to do is read the Bible. Perhaps some brothers and sisters have been reading the Bible in a solid way, but others may not have read the Bible through even once. Therefore, we will speak concerning reading the Bible according to various principles, not from a superficial angle but from a very high perspective.

I believe that many people would answer without hesitation that the Bible is the word of God. However, not too many people have a deep understanding concerning what this means. Even those who have been saved for years may not have a thorough understanding concerning the Bible as the word of God. If we do not have such an understanding of the Bible within us, then we will not be deeply impressed by the Bible.

THE WORD OF GOD BEING GOD HIMSELF

The word of a speaker represents his person. For example, when someone receives a letter from his father and reads it, he does not have the feeling that it is merely a letter from his father, something that is separate from his father; rather, he has the sense that reading his father's letter is the same as seeing his father in person and that he is right in front of his father. This may be likened to reading a letter from the person that we love. When we read it, we sense that it is not just the words of our loved one, but it is as if we are meeting our loved one in person. Hence, words represent the speaker himself, and the word of God represents God Himself. Every time we read the Bible we should have the sense that we are coming not only to the word of God but to God Himself. If we do this, we will be able to read the Bible in a proper way, and the truth we read in the Bible will shine in our inner being. If we take the Bible merely as a kind of teaching, the Bible will not be very profitable to us. Yet every time we read the Bible, if we sense that we are coming to God, this will help us to touch God Himself.

Some people may ask, "Do you have any scriptural basis for saying that the Word of God is God Himself?" Yes, we do. John 1:1 says, "In the beginning was the Word, and the Word was with God, and the Word was God." Verse 14 mentions also that "the Word became flesh." Then 6:63b says, "The words which I have spoken to you are spirit and are life." If we link these three verses together, they will read: "In the beginning was the Word, and the Word was with God, and the Word was God....And the Word became flesh....The words which I have spoken to you are spirit and are life." From these verses we see that the Word of God is God Himself, God expressed, because when the hidden God became flesh, He came as the Word. God is expressed as the Word.

For example, if someone came to visit me at home, and I refused to come out of my room, he would not be able to see me. Yet if I came out but still remained silent, even though he could see me, he would still not be able to touch my person. It is not until I open my mouth to speak that my person really comes out. Once I begin to speak, I am "incarnated," and people are able to touch me. We may use another illustration. Suppose I am really dissatisfied with Brother Tai. This is my inner feeling. Then one day Brother Liu comes to look for me. If I refuse to open the door, he will not be able to see me. Yet when I come out, if he asks me about my impression of Brother Tai, and I remain silent, he will never know what my impression of Brother Tai is until the day that I tell him, "I am really disgusted with Brother Tai." Once I speak this way, my words will represent my very person. Thus, the Word of God not only represents God Himself, but the God who is expressed, not the God who hides Himself.

If in our daily life we met one of our friends, but he would not open his mouth to speak to us, this would be troubling. If a couple had a good talk one night, and the next morning the wife suddenly became silent, this also would be very troubling. The husband would have no way to know what happened within her until he gets her to speak. Once he does, the more she would speak, the more her being and what was happening within her would come out.

The Bible is the word of God, and the word of God is God Himself. The Gospel of John does not say that "God became flesh" but that "the Word became flesh." The entire being of Jesus the Nazarene was the Word of God. If someone were to ask, "Who is the Lord Jesus?", we would tell him that the Lord Jesus is the incarnated God. However, the Bible says that the Word became flesh. The Word who was incarnated is the Lord Jesus; the Lord Jesus, as a whole, is the Word of God. He is the One who speaks forth God. Hence, He said, "The words which I have spoken to you are spirit and are life."

It is not adequate to say that the Lord's words are *of* spirit and *of* life, because actually the Lord's words *are* spirit and *are* life. The entire being of Jesus the Nazarene was the Word of God, the Spirit, and life. God put Himself into His Word, and one day this Word became flesh. This One was Jesus the Nazarene. In this Jesus the Nazarene, there was nothing except the Word of God. The Word of God is God Himself coming forth. The words that came out of Him are spirit and are life. John 1 tells us that the Word was God Himself. Then chapter six tells us that His words are spirit and are life. Since the Bible is the word of God, what does the Bible represent? The Bible represents God Himself. The Lord's words are spirit and are life. Thus, when we read the Bible, we must realize that to know the Bible is to know the Word of God and that the Word of God is God Himself. God Himself, who is Spirit and the source of life, is represented by the Bible. Therefore, the words of the Bible are spirit and are life.

OUR ATTITUDE IN READING THE BIBLE

Having the Right Feeling—
That We Are Coming before God

After we have such a realization concerning reading the Bible, we have to pay attention to our attitude. I am afraid that some brothers and sisters still do not have a thorough understanding concerning what our attitude should be in reading the Bible. A brother once told me of an experiment that he conducted. He placed both a chemistry book and a Bible on his desk. He then spent an hour reading the chemistry book and a second hour reading the Bible. In the end he discovered that according to his inner sense there was a world of difference between these two books. After I heard this, I felt that even such a realization was not adequate. If we could ask the Chinese educator and philosopher, Mr. Hu Shih, about his feeling regarding studying a book on human history versus studying the Bible, he would say that he did not have any particular feeling. He would say that the two books are similar and are both written with Chinese characters. The book on human history has the word *heaven,* and the Bible also has the word *heaven.* The history book contains the word *earth,* and the Bible also contains such a word. The history book speaks of human history, and the Bible speaks of human history as well. He would conclude that these two books are both literary books. This would most likely be the feeling of Hu Shih, and it represents the feeling of non-Christians.

Suppose that today a child of God had a secular book in one hand and the Bible in the other. What would be his sense after having read these two books? In a normal condition, when God's children come to the Word of God, they should have the feeling that they have touched God Himself. When we study chemistry, we touch chemistry; when we study human history, we touch human history. However, when we read the Bible, we should touch God. Hence, I hope that all of us who pursue God would learn this lesson—every time we read the Bible, we should touch God Himself.

For example, this morning someone came to me and told me many things. When he was finished, I had not only heard his words, but I also had touched his person. When a person speaks to us, we not only hear his words but also touch his person. There are many among us who have been saved for years and have read the Bible. However, when we read the Bible, do we touch only the words of the Bible, or do we touch the speaking God? This may be likened to what happens when a person tells us something. Do we have a sense only of his words or of the person who is speaking the words as well? Usually we not only touch the person's words, but we touch also the one who speaks the words. Although we definitely hear their speaking, the one who is speaking is also expressed in his speaking. When his words come forth, his person also comes forth. His word may not give us a very deep impression, but his person should. In the same way, when we read the Bible, we should have the sense that we are touching our lovely Savior. Therefore, every time we read the Bible, we have to exercise to meet God and to touch God.

Take myself as an example. Every time I read the Bible, as long as I contact the word of God, I sense that I have contacted God once again. For instance, even though I may be listening to a certain brother's voice as he is speaking into a microphone, I can still get some impression of that brother and sense his particular flavor. Every time we come to the Bible, we should also sense God's "flavor." We should sense that we have come before God. Those who sense that they have touched God when they come to the Bible seldom come to the Bible as if it were a school textbook, thinking that studying the Bible is similar to studying chemistry or mathematics. It is not so. We must see that as the word of God, the Bible is God Himself coming forth. When we touch the word of God, we touch God.

Having the Right Attitude—
Taking the Word of God as Food

Our attitude when reading the Bible should be similar to the attitude one has when eating breakfast. When we eat breakfast, we do not first analyze which food contains a lot of vitamin A, which food has much vitamin B, how many carbohydrates are in the rice and in the buns, and then determine what to eat first and what to eat next. We do not do this. We have an empty stomach, so we just eat, not paying attention to what contains vitamins or carbohydrates. We simply eat. We do not use our mind; rather, we use our mouth and stomach. Since we know that the Bible is the word of God, the expression of God Himself, and our spiritual food, what should our attitude be when we come to the Bible? Jeremiah 15:16 says, "Your words were found and I ate them." Hence, our attitude toward coming to the Bible should be that we are eating.

Since we should have the attitude that we are eating when we read the Bible, one might ask, "How can we 'eat' the Bible?" Many people have this question. We have to see that the word of God is God Himself and that when God's words come forth, they are spirit and life. Hence, in order to deal with God's word in a proper way and to eat God's word, we must exercise our spirit. We must deal with the word of God by our spirit, not by our mind. We have to read the Bible, contact the word of God, and eat the word of God with our spirit, not merely with our mind. However, what does it mean to read the Bible with our spirit? This is not easy to comprehend. Some people say that to read with our spirit is to read with our inner man, but what does it mean to read with our inner man? Some people may say that this means not to analyze with our mind. We have to spend some time to look into this matter.

When I was young, I studied in a Christian school that promoted the practice of memorizing the Scriptures. At that time I did not know anything except to memorize. This is to read the Bible with the mind. Later when I was around twenty years old, I opened Matthew chapter one and read it again. When I came to Abraham, I studied to find out who Abraham was. Whereas formerly I had used my mind to memorize when reading the Bible, now I used my mind to reason when reading it. However, what does it really mean to read the Bible with our spirit? We all know that the Bible is the word of God and that the word of God represents God Himself. Every time we come to the word of God, we should sense that we are touching God. Since we know that God is Spirit (John 4:24) and that we cannot contact Him with our mind, when we come to God, we should say, "O God, I love You. I come to read the Bible; I come to read Your word." Then perhaps when we open the Gospel of Matthew and come to Abraham, we may ask the Lord, "Who is Abraham?" We may come across many things that we do not understand, but it does not matter if our mind does not understand. Inwardly we will still have the feeling that we have taken a sun bath or that we have been washed with water. Our entire inner being will be refreshed and soothed.

Perhaps some people have had this kind of experience while others have not. As for myself, I have had many experiences like this. In the past when I read the Old Testament, in my mind I often could not understand, but the feeling in my spirit was that I had been washed in the word of God. These experiences were very fresh and soothing. Although I may not have understood the word, still after I read it, my inner being was refreshed. For example, one time I read Daniel 11 and was puzzled concerning the king of the south and the king of the north. Nevertheless, since I had the right attitude—that the word I was reading was the speaking of my beloved Lord—my whole being was brought into the shining of His face, and I felt washed once again. Such a feeling was very fresh, very soothing, and very much a result of fellowship with the Lord. I did not know anything about the king of the south or the king of the north, but deep within my being I felt like I was bathing in God Himself. If we read the Bible in this way, we will sense God's "flavor."

Normally, every saved one should have this kind of experience. Reading the Bible in this way does not mean that we will not retain anything in our memory. For example, when we read Matthew 1, although we may not understand verses 1 through 17, later when we read verse 21, "And you shall call His name Jesus, for it is He who will save His people from their sins," we will understand. We do not read merely with our spirit, but we read with our entire being. We also pray and meditate. After we read the Bible, we will be very much strengthened and refreshed. This may be likened to washing our face with water every morning. When we Christians rise up early in the morning, we should "wash our face" once again in the spirit. With what do we wash our face? We wash our face with the word. The word is the "water," and prayer is the "wash cloth." Normally we wash our face every morning; it would be hard to do this without soap or a wash cloth, but it would be even more difficult to do it without any water.

Many times when a person reads the Word, he may not remember very much, but his spirit is still refreshed by the washing of the Word. Some people say with regret, "After reading the Bible, I forget what I read. What shall I do?" Actually, this is not a problem. Every morning we wash our face, but who can remember the water that we washed our face with? We definitely cannot remember. But it does not matter. Although we may forget the water that we washed our face with, our face was nevertheless washed. Moreover, we do not necessarily forget everything we read. There are two kinds of forgetting. In one kind of forgetting you read the Bible without exercising your spirit, and afterward you forget what you read. This is very poor. Another kind of forgetting is that you read it with your spirit, and afterward you forget. This is not a problem. Every day we should simply exercise our spirit to read the Bible before God and bathe in the shining of His face.

Regrettably, among God's children it is rare to find one out of ten who reads the Bible in such a way. This kind of reading is the wise way. Regardless of how much you understand or comprehend, the most important thing is that you touch God in His word. Although we do not know how to describe what has happened, our spirit truly touches God and the Spirit of God. This is the meaning of taking the word of God as food. It does not matter if we forget what we read. Of course, the things that we learned in our youth are not easy to forget, but when we grow older, we become more forgetful. Twenty years ago when I first began to serve the Lord, two weeks after I released a message, I was still able to recite the entire message to people. But now I cannot even remember the title of the message that I shared on the last Lord's Day. Therefore, we have to study the Bible while we are young.

Having the Right Method—
Finding Out the Main Points
and Contents of the Bible

Concerning the method of studying the Bible, we have heard a lot already. In brief, in order to study the Bible properly we first need to have the right feeling. Next, we need to have the right attitude. Then, we also need to have the right method—memorizing and exploring the word with our mind. In studying the Bible, we cannot totally annul the function of our mind. It would be good if we could memorize at least a few verses. Even though we may not be able to memorize the entire Bible verse by verse, it is still good to memorize the general idea of each chapter. For example, the first section of Matthew 1, from verse 1 through 17, is on Christ's genealogy. The following section is on the birth of the Lord. Chapter two is about the worship rendered by the Gentile magi and the Lord's fleeing to Egypt. Then chapter three mentions the baptism by John. These are the main facts that are worthy of our memorizing and understanding. When we read the Bible, we should use our mind to memorize, understand, and look for the facts; we should not merely read the empty letters.

For example, when we read Matthew 1, we should not just read the letter; rather, we have to find out all the facts in that chapter. When we read Romans 6, we have to know that this chapter is about our co-death, co-burial, and co-resurrection with Christ. Sometimes I ask the brothers which book of the Bible they are most familiar with. After asking a few brothers, no one dares answer my question any more. Even when a brother mentions a book, when I ask him about the main points of that book, he is not able to answer me. This shows us that in our study of the Bible, in addition to exercising our spirit, we have to use our mind to memorize. Once we have memorized the word, it will be easier for us to understand. Then we also have to spend time to search for the facts. Some people seem to know the Bible sentence by sentence and verse by verse, but when all of these sentences and verses are combined together, they do not know what it is all about. Let us use the book of Romans as an example. Chapter one speaks about the sins of the Gentiles. Chapter two speaks about the sins of the Jews. Chapter three speaks about the sins of mankind. Chapter four concerns justification by faith. Chapter five talks about being in Adam. Chapter six speaks about being in Christ. Chapter seven is on being in the flesh. Chapter eight is on being in the Holy Spirit. Chapters nine through eleven cover God's selection and mercy. Chapter twelve deals with consecration. Chapters thirteen through fifteen cover the living of consecration, and chapter sixteen covers the arrangement of some small matters. If we learn all these main points in the book of Romans, the Bible will be very beneficial to us.

I hope we all can see that in reading the Bible we need to find the facts in each chapter. If we can grasp these points concerning having the proper attitude in reading the Bible, we will be able to read the Bible well. We need to have the right feeling and the right attitude, and then we need to find out the facts contained in the Bible. As to how much we should read, we all know that normally if we read one chapter of the New Testament and three chapters of the Old Testament each day, we will be able to read through the Bible once a year. During vacation from work or school, it is best to study a particular book of the New Testament, or sometimes we may also study a specific subject.

STUDYING PROPHECIES, TYPES, AND PARABLES

Prophecies and types are the most difficult matters in the Bible to study. Regarding prophecies and types that are hard to understand, we should not force ourselves to try to expound them. When the prophecy is spoken in plain words, we should understand it according to the plain words. For example, Isaiah says, "The virgin will conceive and will bear a son, and she will call his name Immanuel" (7:14b). We have to interpret this verse literally. As for all the types in the Old Testament, we have to understand them by the explanation of the New Testament and not by our intellect. For instance, the Old Testament refers to the lamb, and in the New Testament John says, "Behold, the Lamb of God, who takes away the sin of the world!" (John 1:29b). Thus, we can know whom the lamb refers to. Furthermore, the Old Testament refers to the bronze serpent (Num. 21:9), and in John 3 the Lord said, "And as Moses lifted up the serpent in the wilderness, so must the Son of Man be lifted up" (v. 14). By this we know that the bronze serpent actually denotes the Lord.

To understand parables we need to study the entire Bible. For example, to understand the parable of the virgins and the oil (Matt. 25:1-13), we first must be familiar with the whole

Bible. If we are, we will be able to realize that the virgins denote Christians, and the oil signifies the Holy Spirit. These are the principles to follow in our study of the prophecies and parables. We must interpret prophecies literally, interpret types with the words of the New Testament, and interpret parables with the entire Bible.

CHAPTER THREE

PREACHING THE GOSPEL

The preaching of the gospel is a simple commission that the Lord gave us before His resurrection and ascension (Matt. 28:18-20). However, in order to preach the gospel in an effective way, there are many things that need to be considered.

BEING DELIVERED FROM SINS

First of all, in order to preach the gospel in an effective way, we must forsake or be delivered from many things. What do we need to forsake, and from what do we need to be delivered? For us to effectively preach the gospel there are at least four things we must forsake or be delivered from. The first thing is sins. If someone wants to preach the gospel powerfully and effectively, he must first get rid of sins in a noticeable way. He may have had some notoriously bad habits or a temper in the past. However, once he is saved and has a desire to preach the gospel, he has to show people clearly that he has been delivered thoroughly from all these things. If he does this, the gospel will go forth from him. If the gospel is not powerful in us, we cannot expect that it will be powerful in others.

Therefore, for a person to powerfully and effectively preach the gospel, he himself must first receive the dynamic gospel of the Lord (Rom. 1:16) that he may be delivered from all his sins and bad habits. If we try to preach the gospel without getting rid of all our sins, temper, and bad habits before the Lord, it will be hard for us to have power in the gospel. For example, if we have a certain habit that our classmates or colleagues look down on, then we should not expect that our gospel preaching will be effective among them. Some brothers and sisters lack power in the gospel because they talk too much. They might be good in all other aspects, but they talk too much. Eventually, all their classmates or colleagues not only disapprove of, but even are disgusted with, their talkativeness. Hence, their gospel is not powerful because their talkativeness has not been dealt with. If their excessive speaking is dealt with, many people will receive their gospel. When we preach the gospel, we have to thoroughly deal with all the things that other people condemn or disapprove of.

This can be compared to Paul's saying that he became all things to all men (1 Cor. 9:20-23). He did this so that he would not offend others. The basic reason for the lack of power in the gospel and for the failure in preaching the gospel lies with us. Many brothers and sisters cannot preach the gospel before men because they have many offenses with which they have not dealt. For example, although they may have offended their classmates or colleagues in the past, now that they are saved they still do not go to them to apologize, to ask for forgiveness, or to make restitution. This is the reason that they do not have power in the gospel. Only when we have thoroughly dealt with all these offenses will we have power in the gospel. This is not only the case with other people, it is the same with our family. We have to absolutely deal with every matter in which we have formerly wronged our parents, husband, or wife. If we have never had a thorough dealing before our family, we should not expect that the gospel will be powerful with them. This is impossible. Only when we have had thorough dealings will we have a powerful gospel.

BEING DELIVERED FROM THE WORLD

Second, in order to preach the gospel effectively, we have to be delivered from the world. Being delivered from the world includes being delivered from our manner of life, our living, and so forth. A gospel preacher should be one who forsakes everything. The more he forsakes, the more powerful the gospel will be. This is why the gospel could be so powerful on the day of Pentecost—the disciples had forsaken everything. Today even though some people have received the outpouring of the Holy Spirit, they still do not have the power of Pentecost.

On the day of Pentecost the disciples forsook all things to follow the Lord, putting aside all of their possessions, reputation, prestige, and family background. Hence, they received power. Of course, whoever receives the Holy Spirit's outpouring will receive power, yet the Holy Spirit will come upon only those who have forsaken all things. The Holy Spirit comes upon us to empower us, but we must be those who forsake all things to follow the Lord. If we have not left all things to follow the Lord, even though the Holy Spirit may come upon us, no power will be manifested. Not only does the Bible tell us this, but church history also confirms this. Every time a person has forsaken everything to follow the Lord, the Lord's gospel has been powerful in him. However, whenever we live a life of ease, we will lose the power of the gospel.

Those who are sent by the Lord to preach the gospel are the Lord's called ones. One time in 1934 we had a time of powerful gospel preaching in Chefoo because all the gospel preachers that day had forsaken the earth and were filled from the heavens. Anyone who has never answered the Lord's call to leave the earth has no way to be filled from the heavens. Every powerful gospel preacher is one who first answers the Lord's call to forsake the earth, who is sent by the Lord, and who is filled from the heavens to preach the gospel to all the nations. Only this kind of person can be powerful in preaching the gospel.

BEING DELIVERED FROM THE SELF

Third, we need to be delivered from the self. To preach the gospel effectively, we need to be delivered not only from our sins and the world but also from the self. Many brothers and sisters lack power in the gospel because they care too much for themselves. Hence, if we want to have power in the gospel, we have to come down from our "throne." Everyone has his own throne—the wife has her throne, the manager has his throne, the student has his throne, the parents have their throne, and the children also have their throne. We all have our thrones, and it is hard for us to come down from them. In short, because everyone has his throne, once they speak just a few words, others can recognize whether they are a wife, a manager, or a university student. However, a powerful gospel preacher is one who is without sins, without the world, and without the self.

Many people are very powerful in the preaching of the gospel, yet they do not have any flavor of the self. You may say that he is a prominent person, yet he does not look like one; you may think that he is a great teacher, but he does not look like one. No one can really tell what he is, because he does not have any airs. Suppose there is a sister among us who is a wife who always sits on her "throne." Surely, this sister's gospel preaching will be powerless. It is the same with those who are students. As long as we desire to keep and preserve ourselves, the gospel will lose ground and power in us. If we want to rise up to preach the gospel, we have to forsake our social position, our prestige, and our self.

Suppose there is a brother among us who is a high school teacher and who has the burden to preach the gospel to people in the countryside. However, these countrymen are nighttime janitors who clean toilets. Will this brother be able to clean the toilets along with them? Most likely he will not be able to do so because he probably has not been delivered from his self. What does it mean to be delivered from the self? In simple words, it means that we do not live in ourselves, but we live "in" others. If you are a high school teacher, when you meet a nighttime janitor who cleans toilets, you will not be in yourself; rather, you will be in him and you will be the same as he. Then you will be able to gain him. Even if you are the wife of a rich man, when you meet the poor wife of a beggar, you will live "in" her and not give her the feeling that she is poor and you are rich. Rather, you will give her the feeling that you are the same as she is. Then you will be able to gain her. I do not have the boldness to say this in other matters, but it is really the case in the matter of the gospel. Suppose some brothers who are managers or bosses say to their subordinates, "You need to be saved. Do not think that it is enough to earn some money every month. If you do not believe in Jesus, you will go to hell after you die." This kind of gospel preaching will have no effect. I saw a sister who told her servant, "You need to believe in Jesus. If you do not believe in

Jesus, you will not be saved. It is terrible to go to hell." This is similar to the emperor of Japan giving an order to his subjects. This kind of a gospel cannot be powerful. To be powerful we have to come out of ourselves.

We cannot say that all of the Western missionaries who came to China in the early days were good, but the majority of them were very good. It is said that there were some missionaries who went to the villages to preach the gospel when they first came to Shantung. At that time many countrymen had lice on their bodies, and even their blankets were full of lice. These missionaries, however, did not mind. When they preached the gospel in the villages, they mixed in with all these countrymen. When they had to stay the night, they shared blankets with these countrymen because the poor people did not have extra blankets. After spending a night with them, the missionaries also had lice all over their bodies. However, because of this they gained many countrymen. Some countrymen were very poor. Outside of their houses they raised hogs, inside their houses they raised donkeys, and in the middle of their houses they had a millstone. At night those who preached the gospel slept within the periphery of the millstone. Beside them were the donkeys, and even at night the donkeys would eat grass. The situation was really miserable. However, each one of them was very willing to suffer. Although today we do not have that many problems in the city, the principle is the same. If we always maintain the attitude that others should accommodate us, the gospel will have no way to go out. Only when we are delivered from the self and accommodate others will the gospel be powerful.

BEING DELIVERED FROM SELF-CONSCIOUSNESS

Fourth, we have to be delivered from our self-consciousness. A gospel preacher should not have any self-consciousness, especially if he is one who preaches from the podium. A person who preaches the gospel from the podium and speaks for God must not be self-conscious. Everyone who preaches the gospel, whether he is preaching from the podium or he is preaching in private, has to lose his self-consciousness. For example, if we preach the gospel to someone on the way to the gymnasium and he is open to receive the gospel, will we be able to kneel down and pray with him at that moment? If we are self-conscious when we kneel down with him, our gospel will not be effective. It is not a matter of having a "thick-skinned" face; rather, it is a matter of simply not having a face. The more we are ridiculed, the more we are "faceless"; the more we are mocked, the more we preach the gospel. Some brothers really have a heart for the gospel, but still they cannot be delivered from their self-consciousness. Hence, even though they do a little preaching of the gospel, they are not released. Thus, power cannot flow out of them.

I believe that our being delivered from these four things—sins, the world, the self, and self-consciousness—will cause the gospel to be powerful. Therefore, we must thoroughly deal with all these matters. In order for the gospel to come out of us in a powerful way, we need to be delivered from these four things. If we hope that our gospel preaching would be powerful, we must carefully deal with these four matters, and the more dealings, the better. This requires us to be "thick-skinned" and even to be "faceless." If we have been delivered from these four things, even without the definite outpouring of the Holy Spirit, we will still have some power.

RECEIVING THE OUTPOURING OF THE HOLY SPIRIT

Fifth, we have to receive the outpouring of the Holy Spirit (Luke 24:49; Acts 1:8). In order to be effective in preaching the gospel, in addition to the dealings related to the four matters mentioned above, we have to pray diligently and exercise our faith to receive the outpouring of the Holy Spirit. The outpouring of the Holy Spirit strengthens our spirit. Without the outpouring of the Holy Spirit, our spirit cannot be fully released. If we want to release our spirit fully, we must have the outpouring of the Holy Spirit. However, without the above four deliverances, the power that comes through the outpouring of the Holy Spirit cannot be manifested. The standard for the outpouring of the Holy Spirit was set on the day of Pentecost. If we want to receive the power of the outpouring of the Holy Spirit, we have to study the situation on the day of Pentecost (Acts 2:1-4). By the day of Pentecost, Peter,

James, and John all had experienced being delivered from various things. No doubt, they were delivered from sins, from the world, and from the self. Moreover, they had no self-consciousness—they had even risked their lives to bear testimony for the Lord. Therefore, the Holy Spirit immediately came upon them. Once the Holy Spirit came upon them, they were empowered. This may be likened to a chemical experiment. Often when a certain element is added to another, tremendous power is produced which induces an explosion. Many people pursue the outpouring of the Holy Spirit and even receive it, yet they are still powerless. Those who received the outpouring of the Holy Spirit on the day of Pentecost had been delivered from certain things. However, today people who pursue the outpouring of the Holy Spirit often have not been delivered from these things. Thus, if we want to receive the outpouring of the Holy Spirit and have powerful gospel preaching, we first need to be delivered from many things.

HAVING ADEQUATE PRAYER

Sixth, we need to have adequate prayer. In the preaching of the gospel, life is crucial, but prayer is even more crucial. Whether we are studying in school or working, if we want the gospel to be powerful with us, we need to gather together and pray to release ourselves, release the gospel, and release the souls of men. The more thorough our prayers are, the more powerful the gospel will be. Our gospel is not powerful because our prayers are not thorough enough. Hence, for us to have a powerful gospel, we must have adequate prayer. In every local church there should be a group of brothers and sisters who are so burdened for the gospel that they pray for the gospel so thoroughly that it seems as if they do not care for anything but the gaining of souls.

HAVING A HEART THAT LOVES THE SOULS OF SINNERS

Seventh, we need to have a heart that loves the souls of sinners. This love is not inherent in us but is given by God; neither does this love come from us, but it comes through prayer. The more we pray for men's souls, the more we will have a heart to love sinners. We will have the feeling that when a sinner's soul is perishing, it is as if we are perishing. The reason why we do not have power in the gospel is that we do not have an adequate concern for people's souls. If we want to be powerful in the gospel, we have to ask the Lord for a heart that loves sinners.

KNOWING HOW TO USE
THE WORDS OF THE SCRIPTURES

Eighth, we have to know how to use the words of the Scriptures. First of all, we need to be delivered from the four items mentioned above. Then we need the outpouring of the Holy Spirit, adequate prayer, and a heart that loves the souls of sinners. Finally, we need to know how to make use of the words of the Scriptures. If we can practice these eight points, our gospel preaching will be very effective. If we have already practiced the above seven points, when we share the gospel with people, we still will need to know how to use the words of the Scriptures. After a person is saved, we still have to nourish and establish him with the words of the Scriptures.

Therefore, we need to be familiar with several categories of truth in the Scriptures and use them precisely. The first category is concerning God, the second is concerning sin, the third is concerning the Savior, the fourth is concerning the way of salvation, the fifth is concerning repentance and believing, and the sixth is concerning the salvation of God. In other words, these few categories are regarding how a person can be forgiven and justified, have eternal life, and be made alive together with Christ. Then the seventh category is concerning the assurance of one's salvation, and the eighth is concerning how a person ought to conduct himself after being saved. We have to be very familiar with all the verses related to these eight categories.

Concerning the Scripture verses for the above eight categories, I have done some arranging. In the first category, concerning God, we may use Romans 1:20 to show people that there is God. Acts 17:24-29 says that men might grope for God and find Him. In addition, Acts 14:15-17 is useful. The verses in this category prove the existence of God. If we can properly make use of these verses, they can be very helpful to us. The best thing to do is to prepare a small notebook and write down all these verses and memorize them, so that we may apply them at any time. The second category of verses is regarding sins. These verses are Romans 3:23, 9-18; 5:12; 6:23; Mark 7:21-23; and Romans 1:28-31. We need to be well versed in these passages concerning sins, or even better, to memorize them. In particular, we should memorize Romans 6:23, which says, "For the wages of sin is death." We have to memorize every word and know the verse references clearly. The third category of verses proves that the Lord Jesus is the Savior. These verses include Acts 4:12; Matthew 1:21; and 1 Timothy 1:15.

The fourth category is concerning the way of salvation—the cross. These verses include 1 Peter 2:24; 3:18; 2 Corinthians 5:21; Isaiah 53:6; John 1:29; Hebrews 9:22; and Matthew 26:28. The fifth category is regarding repentance and believing, which is the way to receive salvation. Mark 1:15; John 3:16, 36; Acts 2:38; and 16:31 can be used. The sixth category is about salvation, which includes forgiveness of sins, justification, having eternal life, and having peace. The verses for this category are Acts 10:43; Isaiah 1:18; 1 John 1:9; Romans 3:28; John 6:47; 5:24; and 1 John 5:12. The seventh category is regarding one's realization of his salvation. These verses include Romans 10:9-10, 13; 1 John 5:13; John 3:36; and 5:24. The eighth category is about one's living after salvation. For this category we can use Mark 16:16 and Matthew 3:8. We have to familiarize ourselves with all the verses of these eight categories.

QUESTIONS ON THE GOSPEL

Question: The brothers do not want us to pay too much attention to man's emotion, but when we preach the gospel, should we put some emphasis on man's emotion and try to touch man's emotion? Should we also use our own emotion?

Answer: Preaching the gospel is not a matter of whether or not we should touch man's emotion. The fact is that man has a spirit and a soul within him and that the major part of the soul is the emotion. Hence, in order for a person to be moved, we must first cause his emotion to be moved. Therefore, when we preach the gospel, we should stir up man's emotion. However, we can do this only to a certain degree. After a person's emotion is stirred, we have to minister the spiritual reality to him. It is useless to merely stir up people's emotions without ministering to them the spiritual realities, because once they leave you, everything will be over. Thus, we have to stir people's emotions to an appropriate degree. Some use too much of their emotion, causing the whole meeting to have an emotional atmosphere, yet there is no solid seed planted into people. As a result, everything is in vain. If a person receives only a kind of excitement yet inwardly does not gain anything substantial, he will remain empty. However, sometimes even though the message itself is excellent, if the seed cannot enter into the ground, it will avail nothing. Hence, we should practice both within limits. We may illustrate this with farming. After we have tilled the ground to a certain degree, we have to sow the seed. Merely tilling the ground is useless; we must also sow the seed. Likewise, it would be futile to sow the seed if the ground were not tilled and loose. Without this, the seed cannot be sowed into the ground. Thus, both must be done in an appropriate manner.

Question: It is usually not so easy for a poor person to preach the gospel to a rich person, or for a "lower-class" person to preach to a "higher-class" person. What should we do?

Answer: It is always difficult for the rich to forget that they are rich and for the poor to forget that they are poor. It is also not so easy for those who have high positions in society to forget their status, or for those who have a low position in society to forget their status. However, for the sake of the gospel, all people should come together, having no consciousness of whether they are rich or poor, highborn or lowborn. When we preach the gospel, we should not have the feeling that we are poor or lowly. Even if we are really poor and of a lowly birth, we should not care. All we care for is the gospel. On the other hand, if we are a rich person or a government official, we should not have pride in ourselves, because our goal is to preach the gospel. When we preach the gospel, we have to be delivered from ourselves so that we do not know what it is to be poor or to be lowly.

Question: If while preaching the gospel we speak too much and our words are too heavy so that the other party has some negative feeling, what should we do?

Answer: We all know that there are two ways to box. The first way is to give the opponent a blow. This way seems rough and heavy, but actually it does not hurt at all. The other way is to hit your opponent in a way that gives the impression that you just barely put your fist on his body. This way does not seem to be heavy at all, but when your opponent takes off his clothes at home, he will find that he has a bruise. It is the same with the preaching of the gospel. Sometimes we have to preach the gospel to certain people in a mild way so that we do not give rise to any negative feelings toward us. We need to practice speaking a heavy word but not in a rough way, just like the second way of boxing.

Question: In our preaching of the gospel, we find that it is harder for the local people, the Taiwanese, to receive the gospel than for the Mainlanders, those who migrated from other provinces of mainland China. What should we do about this?

Answer: The reasons that preaching the gospel to the local Taiwanese is not as easy as preaching the gospel to the Mainlanders are as follows. First, the Mainlanders are easily touched in their emotions to receive the gospel because of their unsettled situation, whereas the Taiwanese are living and working in peace and contentment. Since everything is going well with them, they do not have the heart to receive the gospel. Second, in Taiwan the practice of idolatry is extremely prevailing. Due to their change of environment, however, the Mainlanders have lost their idols, and even their idols have proved to be of no effect. Hence, they are more willing to receive the gospel. Therefore, the brothers should pray much for the spread of the gospel in Taiwan, asking the Lord to bind the strong man, to plunder his goods, and to release the souls of the native people (Matt. 12:29). Third, language is a factor. Those who are from the Mainland do not know the local dialect. Moreover, when some local people are saved, they may not understand the Mandarin that we speak in the meetings. Although we have translation for them in the meetings in which messages are given, we do not have any translation in the prayer meetings or fellowship meetings. This is really hard for them. Several indigenous brothers also said that they can understand only half of the Taiwan dialect and half of Mandarin and that if we were to use Japanese, they could understand everything. Thus, language is really a problem.

Therefore, we need to receive the burden to pray for the native brothers. For the gospel to spread on the island of Taiwan and for us to proceed on this pure path, there should be some native brothers who are raised up by the Lord; ones who have a clear knowledge of the gospel, of the salvation of the Lord, and of the ground of the church, as well as the burden for the gospel. Take the Philippines as an example. In the Philippines we read the Bible in Chinese and speak the Chinese language. Therefore, there is no way for the Filipinos to be saved and brought into the church life. Here in Taiwan, if we could preach, speak, and sing in Taiwanese, or if Mandarin quickly were to become more popular, it would be much easier for the local people to be saved. However, this is not something that can be attained in just two or three years. Therefore, I really hope that some local brothers will be raised up soon who know the Lord's way, have some spiritual experiences, know the ground of the church, and have a burden. Then, with the fellowship and help from the brothers who are from the Mainland, the Lord's testimony will be propagated in Taiwan in a strong way.

Question: We say that when we preach the gospel, we have to completely forget ourselves and not care for our feelings. But if our gospel friend is not willing to listen to us and wants to leave, what should we do?

Answer: A man is wonderful, living, and full of feeling. A man is different from a bench because a bench does not have any feeling. Many times when we preach the gospel, we cannot say that we do not have any feeling. Yes, we do have some feeling, but we need to have wisdom. When others are indifferent and non-responsive, we cannot simply say, "That is fine. If you do not listen to me, I will speak to the bench." Those who preach the gospel from the podium must have the ability to speak something that can draw people's attention and capture them. Once a person is captured he will not think about leaving.

A person's attention is always divided and scattered. Hence, we need to use one or two sentences to arouse his attention and stir him up. This may be likened to fishing. After the fishermen cast their net into the ocean, they pull it in slowly. Some people can use just one or two sentences to capture others and cause them to stay. Once people are willing to stay, we can sow the seed and put something in them. The great evangelist C. H. Spurgeon, who was called by some "The Prince of Preachers," was preaching on the platform one day. He said, "You see, here is a man whose feet have grown into his heart, and whose heart has gone into his feet." Many people were shocked when they heard this, and their attention was drawn. In this way Spurgeon was able to capture people's attention from the very beginning. Then at the end he spoke the gospel into them. Therefore, when we preach the gospel, first we have to stir up people's interest, and then we have to sow the seed of life into them.

Some words spoken on the platform are for touching people's emotion, and some are for enlightening people's mind. However, if the words merely touch man's emotion or enlighten his mind, they still will not work because they are not the words of life. When a person's heart is touched and his mind is enlightened, and even the preacher himself does not use his mind but speaks a few words from his spirit so that they are infused into the person's spirit, this is something of life—the word of life. The effect of touching someone's emotion will pass away quickly, and the effect of enlightening someone's mind will change with the passing of time. However, once life enters into a person's being, it will not go out so easily. It is hard for a person who speaks from the podium to supply everyone's spirit from the beginning of his speaking to the end. On the day of Pentecost there were almost no words that touched people's emotion, and there was only a limited amount of speaking that enlightened people's mind. However, the primary thing that Peter did was to sow spiritual reality into people. In a gospel message that lasts an hour, if we can sow something of spirit and life into people for just ten minutes, this can be considered strong preaching. It takes a farmer much effort to till the ground, but it takes him comparatively little effort to sow the seed. What does it mean to sow the seed into man? When a person's emotion is touched, we sow the words of the gospel into him, not words of emotion or knowledge, but words of life.

Question: When we tell some people about God, they say that we are speaking about some natural phenomenon, and when we tell them that man has a spirit, they say that we are merely describing a psychological phenomenon. What should we do in this situation?

Answer: After we have spoken the truth to a person like this, we have to pray for them. We need to learn to pray for specific people. After we have prayed adequately, we can pray in a stronger way, saying, "O God, we ask You to stretch out Your hand to do something in him." We have to understand that everyone who gives excuses is deceiving himself. Almost all excuses are not the real situation. We have to know that the real situation is one thing while excuses are another. It is easy for men to hide the real situation by giving excuses. They not only cheat others but also deceive themselves. Thus, we should not believe their excuses unless we see that what they are saying is the real situation, because men always express their reasoning according to their own mind.

For example, suppose there are two brothers who are arguing with each other. The real situation is that they are arguing. Yet if these two brothers are not enlightened to see the fact that they are arguing, but only see their reasons for arguing, they will continue to argue. If we want to help them, we have to pray for them: "O Lord, save them from all of their reasonings. No matter how reasonable their argument is, it needs to be condemned." The more we reason, the more we justify ourselves. If we cannot help them by this ordinary prayer, we need a stronger prayer, saying, "O God, we ask You to stretch forth Your hand to break their reasoning." Amazingly these two brothers then may become sick. When others ask, "Why are they sick?", no one will be able to find the cause. At that time we would have to tell them, "Brothers, even though the doctor cannot find out the cause of your sickness, your sickness is still a fact." In this way, they will be enlightened.

Therefore, when we preach the gospel, if someone tells us that what we are speaking about is but a natural or psychological phenomenon, we should not be affected by them; rather, we should pray. Then if he becomes sick, we will tell him that regardless of whether it is a natural phenomenon or a psychological phenomenon, his sickness is a fact. Although we cannot persuade him to believe in the Lord by our speaking, we can pray for him until he believes. Hence, we have to pray in a particular way for some specific ones. When these ones are saved, many others will follow and the gate of the gospel will be opened wide.

CHAPTER FOUR

BEING IDENTIFIED WITH THE DEATH AND RESURRECTION OF CHRIST

Romans 8:3 says, "For that which the law could not do, in that it was weak through the flesh, God, sending His own Son in the likeness of the flesh of sin and concerning sin, condemned sin in the flesh." Moreover, Romans 6:5-6 says, "For if we have grown together with Him in the likeness of His death, indeed we will also be in the likeness of His resurrection, knowing this, that our old man has been crucified with Him in order that the body of sin might be annulled, that we should no longer serve sin as slaves." Furthermore, verses 8-11 go on to say, "Now if we have died with Christ, we believe that we will also live with Him, knowing that Christ, having been raised from the dead, dies no more; death lords it over Him no more....So also you, reckon yourselves to be dead to sin, but living to God in Christ Jesus." These verses show us that Christ is the centrality of God.

God's center and purpose in the universe is Christ. Although this purpose was not plainly written but hidden in a mystery, it is obvious that God's intention and purpose is Christ. Hence, Christ is God's centrality, God's purpose, and God's mystery (Col. 2:2). One day God removed the veil and showed us this mystery, the revelation of God. This revelation is Christ. This revelation is not related to religion but is of Christ. The revelation is not that if we practice religion properly, we will have no problem; rather, it is that when we are in Christ and have no problem in our relationship with Him, we truly will have no problem before God. Everything hinges not on religion but on Christ. Therefore, we must spend much time and effort to know who Christ is.

If we read the New Testament carefully, we will see that all the fullness of the Godhead dwells in Christ bodily (v. 9). Christ is God Himself; He is God (Rom. 9:5; John 1:1). One day He became flesh and came into the midst of mankind, yet within Him was the very God. All the fullness of the Godhead dwells in Christ. The Bible speaks much concerning this. We cannot find God or possess God outside of Christ. All that God has is in Christ. Who is Christ? Christ is God's dwelling place. Moreover, the Bible also reveals to us that when God was incarnated, He put on the flesh. Christ is God, but one day He came to the earth and put on humanity. This is the Word becoming flesh (John 1:14). The Word is God, and flesh is man. Also, Romans 8:3 tells us that when Christ was sent to the earth, He became flesh; that is, He came in the likeness of the body of sin, the likeness of the flesh of sin. When the Lord Jesus became flesh, He put on the body of sin, the flesh of sin. In other words, He was God putting on humanity.

CHRIST BEING THE INCARNATED GOD

Christ was the incarnated God; He was God putting on the flesh. In Him one could meet God, and in Him one could also meet man. Everything of God was in Him, and everything of man was upon Him. He was the mingling of God and man. Everything of God dwelt in Him, and everything of man hung upon Him. Hence, in Him was God's fullness, God's glory, God's life, God's nature, and everything of God. At the same time, He also put on the flesh of man. Hence, man's weakness, man's body of sin, and everything of man were upon Him. Even though He put on man outwardly, inwardly He was without sin (2 Cor. 5:21). Although He did not have the sins of the flesh, He did have the likeness of the flesh of sin. All the problems of man were put on Him. When He was on earth, outwardly He was the same as all men. But on the day that He went up to a high mountain and the God of glory was manifested from within Him, Peter, James, and John saw in Him the glory of God (Matt. 17:1-2). Therefore, we all should be very clear that Christ was the God of glory putting on humanity. Everything of God was in Him, and everything of man was upon Him. He was God yet man.

CHRIST'S DEATH SOLVING MAN'S PROBLEMS

One day this Christ, who was God yet man, went to die on the cross. There on the cross the flesh, the humanity that He had put on was crucified. This is a great mystery. Even though inwardly we may have a deep realization, outwardly we do not have the proper utterance to express this. Christ was God mingled with man. Whatever is of God is glorious, but whatever is of man is problematic. Everything in Christ that was of God was glorious, holy, spiritual, and of life. But the human elements in Christ were all problems, not only concealing the glory of God but also hindering the life of God from being expressed.

One day Christ was put to death on the cross with His human body, with the humanity He had put on. What was crucified was nothing other than the humanity He had put on. As a result, the problem of the flesh, which He put on in His incarnation, was solved on the cross. Christ's death dealt with the flesh and the humanity that He had put on and also released God's life—the glorious life—from within Him. On the one hand, the death of Christ on the cross solved all the problems of man, dealing with all the things of man that had become problems to man. On the other hand, the death of Christ released God with everything of God and of the Spirit from within Him.

CHRIST'S RESURRECTION
RELEASING THE LIFE OF GOD

What a wonderful story this is! When Christ, as the incarnated God who put on humanity, was crucified on the cross, on the one hand He crucified the humanity He had put on, and on the other hand He released the God who was in Him. This is the sum total of Christ's death and resurrection. We have said before that Christ is the mingling of God and man. Then, what is Christ's death? And what is Christ's resurrection? Christ's death terminated everything of man while Christ's resurrection released everything of God. Everything of man was dealt with and everything of God was released—this is the death and resurrection of Christ. Regrettably, among

God's children today, very few have been enlightened by God and have had their eyes opened to see that the Christ whom they have received is such a Christ. Let me ask again, who is Christ? Christ is the One in whom God and man converged and were mingled together. What is Christ's death? Christ's death is the termination of everything of man that He had put on. And what is Christ's resurrection? Christ's resurrection is the release of all the fullness of God that was in Him.

Christ is the One in whom God and man converged. God is glorious and holy, whereas man is sinful, evil, and full of troubles and problems. Yet such a humanity which is subject to troubles and problems was put on Christ as the God who is glorious and holy. This Christ is the mingling of God and man. When the Lord Jesus was walking on the earth, within He had God's nature with God's glory and God's life, and without He had man's body of sin. Inwardly, He was God with the holy and glorious life of God; outwardly, He was a man with the body of sin—He had put on the man of humiliation. In such a situation, what did He do? How was the sinful man without dealt with so that the glorious God within could be released? We can liken this situation to placing a treasure, such as ointment, into a base vessel and then being unable to get it out. The solution would be to break the outer vessel so that the ointment, the inner treasure, could be released. When the Lord Jesus was on the earth, the treasure that was within Him was God Himself and the outward base vessel was man's body of sin. God put Himself into a difficult situation. As the God of freedom He confined Himself in a man so that seemingly He could not get free. One day, however, He was crucified, and the humanity that He had put on was also crucified. Man was completely dealt with on the cross. Then He resurrected, and in resurrection He released everything of God that was within Him.

In His resurrection Christ became the Spirit (1 Cor. 15:45b). As such a Spirit He is omnipresent. He enters as life into anyone who calls on Him and believes in Him. When He as the Spirit enters into a person and lives in that person, immediately that person receives Him and His life, and he is joined to Him as one spirit (John 20:22; 1 Cor. 6:17). At this time, His death becomes that person's death and His resurrection becomes that person's resurrection, because that person has been joined to Him (Rom. 6:5).

When we preach the gospel, we usually tell people that the Lord Jesus died for us to bear our sins. But what is the meaning of the death of the Lord Jesus? The death of Christ, who was God yet man, dealt with all human elements and human problems. Praise the Lord that we have been saved. Christ has come into us and has joined us to Himself so that His death, which dealt with all of our human elements, becomes our death. When we are joined to Him, we are also joined to His death. Romans 6:5a says, "We have grown together with Him in the likeness of His death." His death deals with all of our human elements, such as our pride, our temper, our naturalness, and our flesh. His death specifically deals with everything that comes out of man.

This is the revelation of Christ. He not only died but also resurrected. His death dealt with everyone who belongs to Him. After we are saved, His life comes into us, and as the Spirit He lives in us and is joined to us. Hence, His death has dealt with us. The whole New Testament tells us that the self, the old man, and the old "I" of a person who belongs to the Lord have been crucified with Christ (v. 6; Gal. 2:20). When Christ died, we died with Him in His death. Thus, the Christian faith declares that on the cross our Savior Christ has dealt with all those who belong to Him; the salvation of God tells us that we have been dealt with on the cross. This is truly a tremendous matter in the universe.

Although the Bible tells us that all those who belong to the Lord were already terminated on the cross, do we really know that we too have been terminated on the cross? Do we believe that the death of Christ has already terminated us? I am afraid that not many people have such a realization. This is why we do not have a strong sense that we have been terminated already. Suppose a group of people had all been executed and terminated. Can you imagine how serious a thing this would be? If someone were to ask us, "Do you belong to the Lord? Do you know that you have been crucified with the Lord Jesus?" We might say, "Yes, we belong to the Lord, and we have been crucified with the Lord Jesus," yet we may not have any feeling at all about this. If we really have seen this vision inwardly, our meetings will have a different atmosphere and our living will be different. The northerners will have been dealt with and the southerners also will have been dealt with. Those who are from Canton will have been terminated, and those who are from Shantung also will have been terminated. This is an earth-shaking matter!

Because Christians do not see who Christ is and what the cross is, today's Christianity has become a degraded religion. Regardless of how much religious education we have received or how many religious concepts we have, if we really see that we have already been executed, we will no longer have any religious concepts. This will not be possible. Only those who take Christ as a religion will bring their religious concepts with them. This only proves that they have never been dealt with by the cross. If they were really under the death of the cross and were executed by the cross, they absolutely would not bring their religious concepts into the church. If we have truly been executed by the death of the cross, when we go to Kaohsiung, we would not bring our religious concepts to the church in Kaohsiung. If among us we still have some religious concepts, this shows that we have not seen the death of the cross—we have not seen that we have been identified with the Lord in His death, that we have been crucified with Christ, that we have been executed in Christ, and that we are finished. Because we have been identified with Christ, His death generates the effect in us of putting to death everything that comes from us or belongs to us.

Therefore, in this Savior, with whom we have been united, not only is there death but there is also resurrection. In whomever Christ's death operates, in him Christ's resurrection will also operate (2 Cor. 4:11). Romans 6:8 tells us that if we have died with Him, we believe that we will also live with Him. If we have truly seen that we have died with Christ, this experience of co-death will immediately operate in us, enabling us to experience Christ's resurrection. Christ's resurrection releases both God's life and nature. Through Christ's death everything of man has been dealt with; through Christ's resurrection everything of God has been released. Once we are saved, we are identified with Christ and His death. Once we see this identification, we will immediately declare that we have died with Christ. As a result, all thoughts, persons, and teachings will lose ground in us because in Christ we have died and been dealt with. No method in the whole world is as thorough as death in solving man's problems. All the problems that we cannot solve by any other means are solved upon our death.

Most likely all of us have had the experience of losing our temper and then of being very bothered and wishing that the problem of our temper would be dealt with as soon as possible. The best way for us to deal with our temper, however, is to die. Once we are dead, we will not lose our temper anymore. The only way for us to be a husband or wife who does not lose his or her temper is to die. Neither Confucius, Socrates, nor Wang Yang-ming can help us to solve the problem of losing our temper. The best solution is death. Some sisters are bothered by their talkativeness and have made up their mind again and again not to speak excessively. However, when a situation arises, their mouth is out of their control. There are too many stories like this. The only solution is death. Death solves all the problems. Whether it is a problem in our family with our spouse and children, or a problem in our company with our colleagues, the only solution to all of our problems is death. When we die, everything is finished and all our troubles are gone. Opium smoking is a serious addiction. In order to get rid of such an addiction, there is no other way except death. Death is a big release and is the best solution. Do not think that death deals only with the negative or bad things. In fact, death deals not only with bad things but also with good things, things that are considered positive, such as our meekness, our love, our humility, and our patience. As long as these things are of the self, they will be finished upon our death.

CHRIST WITH HIS DEATH AND RESURRECTION
BEING COMPLETE SALVATION

In Christ's salvation there is the element of death. Complete salvation comprises Christ, His death, and His resurrection. The death of the Lord Jesus and His resurrection constitute complete salvation. The salvation that God gives us is Christ plus His death and resurrection. Every saved one has received Christ, and everyone who has received Christ is identified with Him. Moreover, to be identified with Christ is to be identified with His death and His resurrection. Romans 6 clearly mentions that all of us who have been baptized into Christ Jesus have been baptized into His death and have been buried with Him (vv. 3-4). If through baptism we died and have been buried and raised with Christ, does this mean that we are really dead? Yes, we are dead. It is true that we may know that we have been baptized into Christ's death, but we still may not have been inwardly enlightened to receive the revelation that Christ's death is actually our death. In 1930 I was baptized and died with Christ, but not until 1933 did God show me that I had been crucified with His Son and was already terminated and done away with in Christ. Both the evil and the good in me have been terminated. I have been terminated in Christ's death. His death is my death.

The death of Christ is a great item in His salvation. All that comes out of man and everything that belongs to man, sin, the old creation, the flesh, the world, and Satan have been dealt with through Christ's death. Nevertheless, where His death is, there also is His resurrection. He died, but He was also resurrected. Through His resurrection everything that belongs to God has been released. Only those who have seen Christ's death and resurrection can live in Christ. They see that Christ's death has already dealt with them, and at the same time they also see that the resurrection life of Christ dwells in them for the glory of God to be expressed through them. Once they see this death and resurrection, they are delivered from themselves and live in God. This is God's revelation, this is service with revelation, and this is absolute deliverance from religious concepts.

Suppose that we all are clear about Christ's death and resurrection and a brother comes to us and says, "The church ought to be such and such. It ought to be exceedingly zealous and do many good works." After hearing these suggestions we should first ask, "Brother, when you say these things, are you hanging on the cross or have you jumped down from the cross?" The question here is whether or not our concepts have passed through the death of the cross. Have we passed through the dealing of the cross? Are we those who are truly hanging on the cross, or have we jumped down from the cross? Only those who have experienced the cross can express something of Christ. Whatever has not passed through the dealing and death of the cross is something of man, of the natural being, and of the old creation. These things may be good in man's eyes, but they are not of God.

What are the things that are of revelation, and what are the things that are of the natural being? What are the things that are of God, and what are the things that are of religion? Here is the big test. Have we received the breaking of the cross? How much have we been worked on by the death of the cross? Objectively speaking, Christ is one with His death and resurrection, yet subjectively speaking, how do we experience Christ? To experience Christ is to see His death and resurrection and to live in His death and resurrection. Since we are those who belong to Christ, God will open our eyes to show us that all that is out of us has been hanged on the cross—even our entire being has been hanged on the cross. Everything we are has already been dealt with on the cross. When we see this, we will be able to say, "I have been crucified with Christ. The 'I' with its religious concepts has been crucified with Christ, and now it is no longer I who live but Christ who lives in me. I do not know what religion is, what it is to sin, or what it is to do good; I have already died to all these things. Now it is no longer I who live, but it is Christ who lives in me."

When we see and know that it is no longer we who live but Christ who lives in us, then when we encounter a certain matter, we will test ourselves and ask if we are on the cross or if we have come down from the cross. We will immediately be clear about what has its source in religion and what has its source in revelation, and about what has its source in the natural man and what has its source in God. The focus of God's salvation is not the original goodness or evilness of man;

rather, the emphasis of God's salvation is that the original man has been dealt with on the cross. Moreover, it is that God has gained the ground in this man who has been dealt with on the cross. This is absolutely not a matter of religion, nor even of Christianity; it is a matter of Christ. The cross dealt with man, and resurrection released God. Christ's death dealt with our human element, and Christ's resurrection released God's element to the fullest extent. The more we pay attention to Christ's death and resurrection, the more we will touch the spiritual things and be before God. If we do not pay attention to Christ's death and resurrection, then regardless of how much people praise us, we still will have too much of our fallen human element. Hence, in our daily living we have to pay more attention to our identification with Christ's death and resurrection.

CHAPTER FIVE

HUMAN OPINIONS VERSUS
RESURRECTION POWER

Matthew 16:15 records that the Lord asked the disciples, "Who do you say that I am?" Simon Peter answered and said, "You are the Christ, the Son of the living God" (v. 16). Then Jesus said to him, "Blessed are you, Simon Barjona, because flesh and blood has not revealed this to you, but My Father who is in the heavens" (v. 17). Following this, the record in verses 21-24 tells us: "From that time Jesus began to show to His disciples that He must go to Jerusalem and suffer many things from the elders and chief priests and scribes and be killed and on the third day be raised. And Peter took Him aside and began to rebuke Him, saying, God be merciful to You, Lord! This shall by no means happen to You! But He turned and said to Peter, Get behind Me, Satan! You are a stumbling block to Me, for you are not setting your mind on the things of God, but on the things of men. Then Jesus said to His disciples, If anyone wants to come after Me, let him deny himself and take up his cross and follow Me." The things recorded in this portion of the Word do not fit in with our human concepts, but they are part of the divine revelation.

SEEING CHRIST IN ORDER TO SEE
THE REVELATION OF GOD

Many people do not know what the revelation of God is. Actually, the revelation of God is nothing but Christ revealing Himself. If a person wants to know the revelation of God, he must know Christ. In fact, the revelation of God is Christ. Only when we see Christ will we be able to see the revelation of God, and only when we know Christ can we be those who live in the revelation of God.

The revelation of God is His unveiling of Christ for us to see and know. It is God who causes us to see and know Christ. If a person does not see and know Christ, no matter what kind of living he has before God, what kind of things he does, or what kind of behavior he has, they are all outside of God's revelation. We have seen that everything that is outside of God's revelation is of religion and is natural. Only when a person sees and knows Christ will all of his living, doing, and behavior be out of God's revelation.

To many people these words may be hard to comprehend. A clever brother who had a clear mind and who was rich in thought once said that he did not know what God's revelation was. We should not marvel at hearing such a word because man often cannot understand or comprehend the revelation of God. Only when the Holy Spirit gives man the enlightenment and revelation within is man actually able to see, rather than merely understand or comprehend.

For example, suppose that when we come to the meeting hall, all the doors and windows are shut. Suppose also that on our way to the meeting hall we met a person who described to us the interior setting of the meeting hall. He described how many chairs, lamps, fans, and microphones there are and how they are arranged. We then more or less have some idea and understanding of everything in the meeting hall. However, the doors and windows of the meeting hall are shut, the interior setting is concealed and blocked, and we have no way to see inside. We heard the description from the person we met, and seemingly we understood, apprehended, and comprehended, yet because we cannot see the real situation, we are still not clear. Not until the door is opened, we enter the meeting hall, and the lights are turned on will we really understand. This understanding is different from an outward understanding. An outward understanding is based upon hearing about something without having any light or actual seeing. Once the door is opened and the real situation is revealed before our eyes, we will be able to see the meeting hall in a clear way. Such a seeing is a revelation.

We may have these two different kinds of knowledge of Christ. One is the result of hearing someone speak about Christ and about the kind of relationship we should have with Him. Even though the speaker may have given a clear and reasonable presentation, and we heard it clearly, we still find it vague because the Holy Spirit has not yet shown us the actual matter. We merely heard the presentation, but we have not seen it. Hence, we may understand the doctrines concerning Christ, but we may not be able to see or know the Christ who is in us. We may understand the doctrines, but if we do not have any inward seeing, then even though we may think that we know and understand, we still do not really know or understand.

REVELATION OR RELIGION

May the Lord grant us the grace to not only have some mental understanding of Christ but to have the inward revelation and seeing that will cause us to know Christ. Such a knowledge of Christ will affect us inwardly so that our living and daily walk will be directed by the Lord. As a result, our living and daily walk will be according to revelation and not according to religion. Whatever we are able to do without touching Christ or contacting Christ comes out of religion. Only when Christ touches us in our being will what we do be according to revelation.

Suppose a young brother realizes that children ought to honor their parents and, therefore, cultivates his character and disciplines himself so that he can wait upon his parents. Although this is good, this kind of goodness is religious and natural, because even without knowing Christ, without touching Christ, and without Christ being his Lord and directing him inwardly, he is willing and able to do such a thing. What does it mean to do something according to revelation? For this young brother it would mean that after he is saved, he fellowships with the Lord, knows and touches Christ, and has Christ as his Lord reigning in him and restricting him. He gets to know Christ in such a way that Christ directs him from within, causing him to be restrained and under control. He does not resolve to do anything, yet Christ in him regulates him, causing him to discipline himself, submit to his parents, and be an obedient son to them. Such obedience and submission are not of religion or of the natural man but are lived out by this young brother because inwardly he knows Christ, touches Christ, and has Christ reigning in him. The One who is reigning in him is Christ Himself. Christ reigns in him and lives out from him. This is something of revelation.

All of our living and daily walk that we express outwardly that issues from touching Christ and from inwardly being under the influence and control of Christ is according to revelation. All that we do by our own determination and effort without touching Christ, going through Christ, or being controlled by Christ is of religion and of the natural man. This is to do something apart from revelation. In simple words, whatever is the result of revelation is the result of seeing Christ and of His being the Lord within us, reigning over and controlling our being. When this happens, we have a living and behavior that are under His control and authority.

THE CONTENT OF THE HOLY WORD BEING CHRIST

How then can we see revelation? There is a way. In fact, there is a way for doing everything. Once we have found the way, it is easy for us to do something. We know that God reveals Christ to us first by the holy Word and second through the Holy Spirit. Therefore, we need to know Christ and see the revelation of Christ through the Word and the Spirit. We all know that Christ is the content of the Bible and that the entire Scriptures speak concerning Christ (John 5:39-40). God has put Christ in the Word, and if we read the Word properly, we should be able to find Christ in it. This may be likened to putting sugar into water. When we get the water, we get the sugar as well. If we cannot find Christ in our reading of the Bible, we are not reading the Bible successfully. Someone who knew God once said that Christ is in every chapter of the Scriptures. When he read about Adam, he saw that Adam typifies Christ; when he read about Moses, he saw that Moses typifies Christ; and when he read about David, he saw that David also typifies Christ. Whether it is the Old Testament or the New Testament, the whole Bible is full of Christ. God uses different ways, including types, prophecies, and parables, to portray Christ. When we read the Bible, if we merely read the types, the prophecies, or the parables without seeing Christ, then our reading of the Bible will be in vain. To read the Bible properly, we must see Christ in the Bible. Since the content of the Bible is Christ, we are reading the Bible successfully only if we are able to see Christ in every chapter, every verse, and every sentence of the Bible.

THE HOLY SPIRIT IN US BEING CHRIST

Not only is Christ embodied in the Word, but He is also realized as the Spirit. He Himself told us that the Holy Spirit, who is the Spirit of reality, would abide with us and be in us (John 14:17). Strictly speaking, the Holy Spirit's coming into us is Christ's coming into us (v. 20). Some people testify that the Holy Spirit in them gives them comfort, and others say that the Holy Spirit in them gives them knowledge. Having comfort and knowledge is good, but it is not good enough. The central purpose of the Holy Spirit's being in us is to reveal Christ. He leads us and comforts us that we may know Christ. If we merely receive His leading and comfort without seeing or knowing Christ, something is still missing in the leading and comfort we are receiving, because the Holy Spirit in us is Christ.

For example, consider the following story. There was once a diamond that was put into a nice box. Then someone saw the nice box, and he took it away. Eventually, however, because this person did not realize that he had a diamond, he threw it away and kept only the box. Many people are like this. They receive the guidance and the enlightenment of the Holy Spirit without receiving Christ. What is the reason for this? It is because they think that the Holy Spirit in them is only for enlightening and leading them. They do not see that the central purpose of the Holy Spirit's entering into them is that through leading, enlightening, and other kinds of work they may know Christ and gain Christ. Hence, whether it is reading the Word or receiving the leading of the Holy Spirit, God's only purpose is that we may gain Christ. If we receive the leading without gaining Christ, the leading that we receive is in vain.

However, how can we see Christ in the Word? How can we know Christ by the sense of the Spirit? These are truly difficult questions. We will not be able to see Christ in the Word, know Christ by the sense of the Spirit, and therefore solve all our problems merely through a few words of explanation. Here, we can only point out the way. In principle, whenever we read the Bible, we should receive revelation. However, because we have too many of our own views, opinions, and ideas we often cannot see any revelation when reading the Bible. The biggest hindrances to our receiving revelation when reading the Bible are our views, opinions, and concepts. We saved ones all have the Holy Spirit within us. In principle, we all should know Christ because the Holy Spirit is within us revealing Christ to us. Yet many of us do not know Christ because of the problem of our own views and ideas. These are frustrations to the Holy Spirit. Our views and opinions hinder us from knowing Christ.

Here we have to mention two passages. One is Matthew 16, which speaks of the cross of Christ, and the other is John 11, which is concerning the power of Christ's resurrection. In both cases the Lord encountered human frustrations. For instance, one day the Lord Jesus told His disciples that He must go to Jerusalem to be crucified and suffer death. This truly was a revelation. This matter of the Lord's crucifixion was originally hidden, but that day the Lord Jesus revealed this hidden matter to the disciples. The disciples should have understood this. Instead, the Lord encountered someone who had his own opinion. This one's opinion was a good opinion, an opinion of love, yet it was a human opinion. We all should remember the story at the end of Matthew 16. The Lord Jesus told His disciples that He must go to Jerusalem to be crucified and suffer death. Then right after the Lord finished speaking, Peter came in and said, "God be merciful to You, Lord! This shall by no means happen to You!" (v. 22). The Lord Jesus had revealed His crucifixion to the disciples, but Peter did not understand. Was it because he did not love the Lord that he did not understand the Lord's word? It was not that he did not love the Lord but that he loved the Lord so much that he expressed his opinion. He took the Lord aside and told the Lord that this would by no means happen to Him. This prevented Peter from seeing the revelation of the cross.

HUMAN OPINION
FRUSTRATING THE LORD'S REVELATION

Please bear in mind that there are many "Peters" here. With many of us, either we do not love and desire the Lord, or once we do, we have our own views and ideas. No one loves the Lord without his opinion, and no one desires the Lord without his own views and ideas. The strange thing is that when we are indifferent toward the Lord, we simply put the Bible aside and do not read it. However, after we are revived and become zealous, we begin to read the Bible, and in so doing we read everything that is in our mind into the Bible. We are the same as Peter. If the Lord were to have told us that He was going to be crucified, we also would have had our own opinion, view, and idea. We also would have told the Lord, "God be merciful to You. This shall by no means happen to You!" The Lord had His revelation, but Peter had his own opinion. Peter's view frustrated the Lord's revelation.

Many Bible readers cannot see the revelation in the Bible because they are full of their own opinions, views, and ideas. Human beings are really strange in that whether they are well educated or not, they always consider that they are right, and they always have their own views, opinions, and ideas. This is not only the case with educated people but also with less educated people. Even the elderly saints are not an exception. On that day the Lord Jesus' word was very clear, but Peter still did not understand it; he was inwardly resisting it. Why was he unable to receive the Lord's word? He was not able to receive the Lord's word because he had his own views, ideas, and opinions.

Our opinions always frustrate the Lord's revelation. One day a householder wanted to hire a servant. The first servant came, and the master wanted to test him to see if he would listen to his word. He said to the servant, "Please go to the garden and plant this tree upside down with its roots facing upward and its branches facing downward." The master was afraid that the servant did not hear him clearly, so he repeated, "The roots should be facing up and the branches facing down—are you clear?" The servant replied, "I am clear." Then he went to the garden, but when he was about to plant the tree, his opinion came. He thought that the master must have spoken the opposite of what he wanted, for how could someone plant a tree with its roots on top and its branches on the bottom? The more he thought about it, the more he believed that he was right, so according to his own decision, he planted the tree with its roots on the bottom, facing down, and its branches on top, facing up. When he went back to the house, the master asked him, "Did you plant the tree?" He said, "Yes, I did." Then the master questioned him, "How did you plant it?" He answered, "With its roots on the bottom and its branches on top." The master inquired of him, "But what did I tell you?" He replied, "I was afraid that you had misspoken so I planted the tree this way." In the end the householder discharged him. Then a second servant came. The master asked him also to plant the tree in the inverted way, upside down. Again the master feared that the servant had not listened clearly, so he said it again and asked him, "Did you listen carefully?" He answered, "Yes, I did." Then the second servant went to the garden. He considered and reconsidered his master's word and simply could not make any sense of it. He thought that the master must have spoken too quickly and said the reverse of what he intended. Eventually, he also planted the tree with its branches on top and its roots on the bottom. We are the same in our reading of the Bible. Like the two servants, we always read the Bible according to our own way, considering that we are right and thinking that the Bible must mean the opposite of what it says.

PUTTING ASIDE OUR OPINION
WHEN READING THE BIBLE

Although we all know that God's thoughts are higher than our thoughts, and God's ways are higher than our ways (Isa. 55:8-9), many times we still like to use our mind to measure

God's thoughts. It is hard for us to have no opinions when reading the Bible, unless we do not read the Bible at all. We all have the same Bible in our hands, yet the results of our reading are altogether different. What one person reads in the Bible is one thing, and what I read may be another thing. If you do not believe this, we can do an experiment. We can let everyone read the same chapter, the same verse, and even the same phrase. In the end we will all come up with different things. This is because even before we read, we already have our own opinions. We do not simply discover the things in the Bible; rather, we put our own opinions and thoughts into the Bible. We may use an illustration. Water itself is colorless, but if we are wearing a pair of glasses with green lenses, we may insist that water is green. The fact is that it is not the water that is colored but that we looked at it through a pair of colored glasses. Hence, if we want to find Christ and know Christ from the Bible, we must put aside all of our own views and opinions. Then when we read the Bible, we certainly will receive light and revelation from the Bible.

PUTTING ASIDE OUR OPINIONS
IN ORDER TO KNOW CHRIST

If we read John 11, we can see two things. We can see that the Lord already had determined what He would do to Lazarus to manifest His resurrection life with its resurrection power. Yet we can also see that when He went to carry out this matter, the Lord encountered a problem, the problem of human opinions and views. This is a great problem in the Gospel of John. When people read John 11, many of them see the Lord's power but not man's opinions. In fact, there are many human opinions in the Gospel of John. In John 11 we are told that Jesus loved Martha and her sister and Lazarus (v. 5). When Lazarus was sick, the two sisters sent people to Jesus. First of all, the two sisters expressed their opinion in the way that they informed the Lord. How do we know this? They sent people to Jesus to say, "He whom You love is sick" (v. 3). Such a word was full of opinion. The Lord, however, was determined to deal with these human opinions. Hence, after He heard such a word, He remained in the place where He was for two days (v. 6). They wanted Him to come quickly, yet He purposely would not come. They expected that He would come in two hours, but He did not come on the first day; neither did He come on the second day. These two sisters were really suffering a great ordeal because they were full of their own ideas and thoughts. If instead of having their own ideas and opinions they would have just allowed the Lord to come whenever He desired, they would have been freed from having any burden or experiencing any ordeal after they had prayed. However, their prayer was to ask the Lord to come quickly. They were expecting every minute and every second that the Lord would come, yet the Lord did not come on the first day, the second day, or the third day. Even after Lazarus died and began to smell, He still did not come.

Not only did these two sisters have their opinions, but the disciples also were the same. When people told the Lord, "He whom You love is sick; will You go?" He did not go. He was truly the Lord of dealings. When people said, "You should go," He did not go. But two days later, when the disciples had decided not to go, the Lord said to them, "Let us go into Judea again." But the disciples did not agree. The Lord Jesus told them, "Lazarus has fallen asleep; but I am going that I may wake him out of sleep." The disciples replied, "If he has fallen asleep, he will recover." Then the Lord had to tell them plainly, "Lazarus has died." Then Thomas said to the rest of the people, "Let us also go, that we may die with Him" (vv. 7-16). What he meant was that if the Lord was not afraid of being stoned by the Jews and was going to die, then they would go also to die with Him. These were all human opinions.

When the Lord Jesus arrived, Martha went to meet Him. Martha was the active one whereas Mary was the quiet one. When Martha saw the Lord Jesus, the very first thing she said was, "If You had been here, my brother would not have died" (v. 21). Her opinion was correct. Because the Lord came so late, Lazarus had already been buried. She seemed to ask why the Lord still bothered to come. We have to know that all opinionated people have an endless number of things to say. Martha's opinions did not stop here; she went on to say,

"Whatever You ask of God, God will give You" (v. 22). It was quite good that she could speak such a great truth. But if she really knew this, why did she still complain? Then Jesus said, "Your brother will rise again." Martha replied, "I know that he will rise again in the resurrection in the last day" (vv. 23-24). Martha postponed the present resurrection to the last day; this was a difference of two thousand years. Then Jesus said to her, "I am the resurrection and the life" (v. 25a). What the Lord meant was, "You do not need to wait until the last day. Where I am, there is resurrection." Then He continued, "He who believes into Me, even if he should die, shall live....Do you believe this?" (vv. 25b-26). Martha said to Him, "Yes, Lord; I have believed that You are the Christ, the Son of God, He who comes into the world" (v. 27). Basically she did not answer the Lord's question. The mighty resurrected Lord was standing in front of Martha, yet she did not even know Him or understand what He was saying. Why not? She did not know Him or understand what He was saying because of her opinions. After Martha had finished speaking, she went away and secretly called her sister Mary, saying, "The Teacher is here and is calling you" (v. 28). When did the Lord call Mary? Again we see that Mary was very quiet, and Martha was very active. Martha could not hear the Lord's speaking because inwardly she was full of opinions.

Before the Lord Jesus entered into the village, Mary had also come to him and spoken the same word: "If You had been here, my brother would not have died" (v. 32). Up to this point, by the time the Lord could say one sentence, the two sisters had already spoken ten sentences. Martha had opinions, and Mary also had her opinions. There was a whole pile of opinions. Faced with this kind of situation, the Bible tells us that Jesus wept (v. 35). Why did He weep? Did He weep because of the death of Lazarus? No. Did He weep because of the problem facing Martha and Mary? No. He wept because of all these human opinions. The Lord was able to raise the dead. Everyone should have been filled with praises. However, they not only did not understand Him, but they were also full of opinions. Thus, the Lord wept. Today the sufferings we have in our daily life are not real sufferings. The real suffering is that we do not know the Lord. The Lord is truly here, yet we do not know Him. The Lord's word cannot enter into us, and because of this He weeps.

Later, the Lord, being moved with indignation, came to the tomb and charged the people, saying, "Take away the stone" (v. 39a). Even at this moment, Martha was still there expressing her opinion, saying, "By now he smells, for it is the fourth day that he is there" (v. 39b). What she meant was that since Lazarus already smelled, it would be useless to do anything, and the Lord had no need to open the tomb. On the one hand, John 11 shows us that the Lord has the resurrection power; on the other hand, the whole story is full of human opinions. Then the Lord Jesus said, "If you believe you will see the glory of God" (v. 40). Here what the Lord meant was that regardless of the condition of Lazarus or the fact that he smelled, Lazarus would rise again. This shows us that the Holy Spirit is within us for us to know that Christ is living. The biggest frustration to knowing Christ in such a way is that we have too many opinions. It is because of our opinions that the Lord's power cannot be expressed and that we cannot know Him. Too often we judge matters only according to our own views and opinions. The reason why the Lord's resurrection life and glory often cannot be expressed through us is that we have too many opinions. In brief, in order to know Christ and follow Christ, we must put aside all of our views and opinions.

CHAPTER SIX

THE REVELATION OF JESUS CHRIST

THE REVELATION OF CHRIST

Galatians 1:11-12 says, "For I make known to you, brothers, concerning the gospel announced by me, that it is not according to man. For neither did I receive it from man, nor was I taught it, but I received it through a revelation by Jesus Christ." The gospel came to Paul, that is, it was received by Paul, through a revelation of Jesus Christ. Here the apostle shows us one thing—the revelation of Jesus Christ. This is not merely a revelation received through Jesus Christ but a revelation concerning and belonging to Jesus Christ Himself.

Verses 15-16 continue: "It pleased God...to reveal His Son in me." Moreover, Colossians 2:2b-3 says, "The mystery of God, Christ, in whom all the treasures of wisdom and knowledge are hidden." Verse 9 says, "For in Him dwells all the fullness of the Godhead bodily," and 1:26-27 reads, "The mystery which has been hidden from the ages and from the generations but now has been manifested to His saints; to whom God willed to make known what are the riches of the glory of this mystery among the Gentiles, which is Christ in you, the hope of glory." Furthermore, Ephesians 3:3-5 says, "That by revelation the mystery was made known to me, as I have written previously in brief, by which, in reading it, you can perceive my understanding in the mystery of Christ, which in other generations was not made known to the sons of men, as it has now been revealed to His holy apostles and prophets in spirit." All these verses show us that there is something that has never come up in our mind and does not exist in our mind. The Chinese do not have it, and in fact, everyone in the entire world other than those who have been enlightened by God do not have it. What is it that none of these people have? It is the revelation of Christ.

There is something in this universe called the revelation of Christ. The meaning of the word *revelation,* not to mention the phrase *the revelation of Christ,* is hard for us to understand. If we ask the saints what *revelation* means, I believe only a few could give us its meaning. The revelation in the Holy Scriptures is not merely the revelation of the things contained in the Holy Scriptures, but even more it is the revelation of Christ. Moreover, the word *revelation* itself indicates that this is something that has never occurred to our mind nor come up in our heart.

REVELATION BEING THE OPENING OF A VEIL TO SHOW US SOMETHING

It is really profitable for us to spend some time to see what a revelation is and to proceed further to see the revelation of Christ. Literally, the word *revelation* in Greek means the opening of the veil on a stage. We all know that before a show begins, the stage is completely covered with a veil and that people can see only this veil. When the show begins, the veil covering the stage is gradually opened. Revelation is the opening of the veil in order to show us something. In the past something was hidden from us, and there was a veil separating us from that thing. But now the veil is opened to show us the real situation behind the veil. This opening is a revelation.

The Lord Jesus is truly a mystery, and the whole universe is a mystery. Throughout the world people who are somewhat thoughtful know that the universe is a mystery. Philosophers throughout the ages still have not been able to explain to us what the universe really is. Why is there a universe? Why are there so many different kinds of things in it? Why are there human beings? For what purpose do they exist? What is the meaning of human life, and what is the purpose of our living? Not only did the Chinese sages find it difficult to answer these questions, but even the Western philosophers have no answers for them. Neither Confucius nor Socrates knew the answers. Even godly people in the Bible such as Elijah, Jeremiah, David, Moses, and Abraham did not know. They only knew that there is a sovereign One in the universe and that this sovereign One is Jehovah God, the unique and true God who created the heavens, the earth, everything within the heavens and the earth, and mankind. This was all that the prophets, the ancient saints, and the past sages knew.

THE MYSTERY OF GOD BEING HIDDEN IN THE GOD WHO CREATED ALL THINGS

The ancient saints and the past sages throughout history have no answer to the questions: What is the purpose of God in creating the heavens and the earth? Why did He create mankind? Some people may ask, "Are we too much in saying this?" We are not too much in saying this. We do have the scriptural basis. Both Ephesians and Colossians tell us clearly that God has a hidden mystery. We all know that a mystery is something that is not manifested or made known to others. For example, when a speaker is standing at the podium, we know that he is going to preach and speak. However, if he keeps his mouth shut while he is standing there, we have the sense that he is a mystery. We cannot hear anything from him; we can only see him standing there with his mouth shut. This is his mystery.

Our God also has a mystery. This phrase, *the mystery of God,* is found in Colossians 2:2. Ephesians also tells us that this mystery is one that was hidden in God (3:9). God hid this mystery in Himself and did not tell anyone about it. Moreover, this God who hid the mystery in Himself is the God who created all things. Hence, this mystery was hidden in God, who created all things. This is recorded in Ephesians 3. In reading the Bible, most people can easily find speaking concerning things like humility, patience, and peace, but they cannot easily see the speaking concerning the mystery of God. Ephesians 3:9 says, "And to enlighten all that they may see what the economy of the mystery is, which throughout the ages has been hidden in God, who created all things." Please notice that this mystery was hidden in God and that He is the

One who created all things. Thus, this mystery was hidden in God, who created all things.

Verses 3 through 5 read, "That by revelation the mystery was made known to me, as I have written previously in brief, by which, in reading it, you can perceive my understanding in the mystery of Christ, which in other generations was not made known to the sons of men, as it has now been revealed to His holy apostles and prophets in spirit." This reveals that God had a mystery. Although He created all things and man, He did not tell man of this mystery. It was not until the New Testament, when the apostles and prophets came, that He revealed it to them. These prophets were not of the Old Testament but of the New Testament. Although they knew that all things were created by God, they did not know God's purpose for creating all things.

Even in the New Testament age there are still many people who do not know why God created the heavens, the earth, and man. Until this day it is still a mystery to many people. Although they have their religious thoughts, concepts, and living, and although they also worship and serve God, their service is not something of revelation but is something of religion. They are completely ignorant of God's purpose. What is man? Why does God save man? Is His intention merely for man to enjoy peace today and go to heaven in the future? All these thoughts are religious concepts. Please bear in mind that God does not save us merely for us to enjoy peace; rather, He saves us for a purpose hidden in Himself.

THE MYSTERY OF GOD BEING CHRIST

There is indeed a mystery hidden in God. For example, why did God create the universe? Why did He create mankind? Why did He create all things? Initially, He did not tell anyone about all these things. God hid this purpose in Himself, so it became a mystery. He created the heavens, yet the angels in the heavens did not know why He did it. He created the earth, yet the people on the earth also did not know why He did it. Throughout the ages there were many prophets, but He never told any of them the purpose of His works; He never told anyone. Then what is this mystery?

What is the purpose of God? Colossians 2:2 tells us, "The mystery of God, Christ." God's purpose is Christ. God created the universe for Christ. God created mankind for Christ. God created everything for Christ. Everything of God is for Christ.

Today God is still working because He has not yet obtained His purpose. When all things are headed up in Christ, then the work of God will be fully accomplished. Ephesians 1:10 says, "Unto the economy of the fullness of the times, to head up all things in Christ, the things in the heavens and the things on the earth, in Him." This word says clearly that at the fullness of the times all things will be headed up in Christ. It is because all things are for Christ that God created the universe, it is because all things are for Christ that God created man, and it is because all things are for Christ that God created everything. God's purpose is for Christ, and God's purpose is Christ. Hence, the mystery of God is certainly Christ.

The Chinese sages and the Jewish prophets did not know this mystery. Even Paul, who had been taught by a great rabbi, originally did not know it. Yet one day God opened the veil to Paul, and he immediately saw something—he saw Christ. This is a revelation, a revelation unveiling Christ. Before God revealed Christ, there was a veil covering the universe. There was such a thing as the purpose of God for which God created the universe and mankind, but this purpose was hidden and not seen until the New Testament age when Christ came and was manifested for men to see. When the Holy Spirit opened the veil, Christ was seen by men. Now that we can see everything clearly, we realize that the story of the universe is the story of Christ. It is not a matter of whether or not we worship God but a matter of whether or not we have Christ.

I hope that we all will see the revealed Christ. The revealed Christ is none other than the hidden Christ who revealed and unveiled Himself. Who is this Christ? This Christ is God Himself, the God who became flesh. If we are not in Christ, even though we may say that we are serving God, in actuality we cannot serve God because God is not in our service. Originally this was Paul's situation. He seemed to be zealously serving God, yet he was actually opposing God. Hence, we need to see that the mystery of God is Christ. One day God opened this mystery to man. This opening is the revelation of God, and this revelation shows Christ to us. So what is revelation? When man touches and contacts God in Christ, this is revelation.

We have been deeply influenced by religion, yet we are very shallow concerning the revelation of Christ. Even young brothers and sisters, not to mention those who are in their seventies or eighties, have religious concepts. Many young people believed in the Lord and were baptized, but they have less of the element of Christ in them than they do of religion. If we speak with them, we will find that they all have an idea of what it means to serve God. They already have a picture in their minds of what it is to serve God before they have read the Bible or listened to a message. For example, their mind is already filled with many religious concepts regarding how to be a Christian and how to treat the saints. In fact, we are all filled with religious concepts but short of revelation. After being saved, there is not a single person who serves God in the church without having a set of religious concepts. The Chinese have the Chinese concept, the Americans have the American concept, the Japanese have the Japanese concept, and the Indians have the Indian concept. Furthermore, the males have the male concept, and the females have the female concept. We all came into the church with a set of concepts regarding serving God. If we had these concepts before even reading the Bible, where do they come from? This is a mystery that no one can explain. Every saved person has certain concepts regarding how to be a Christian and how to conduct himself in the church. These concepts are nothing more than man's own concepts.

The kind of person we are determines the kind of Bible we read. When the Chinese read the Bible, they say that the Bible is really good because it talks about loyalty, filial piety, kindness, love, propriety, justice, honesty, and a sense of shame. When the Indians read the Bible, they also say that the Bible is really good because it teaches man to suffer. One day a sister came to me and said, "In recent days my husband, who is also a Christian, has been very cruel to me. Having come to my end, I went to read the Bible and eventually found a teaching saying that husbands ought to love their wives" (Eph. 5:25). She then thought that the best Christian is one who loves his wife. This shows us the concept that was in her mind. She already had within her three words, "love your wives," even before she began to read the Bible. Hence, when she came to the Bible, she could not see anything else. However, once she read the words "love your wives," these three words seemed to be magnified. All these cases show us that the kind of person we are determines the kind of Bible we read.

For instance, I once knew a meek person. One day he came to me and joyously said, "According to the Bible a meek person is the best, because among the nine blessings, there is one concerning the meek." In Tsingtao I met a harsh brother. He said, "These days I have been seeing the light that sometimes we should not be too polite or gentle, because even the Lord Jesus Himself used a whip one day to drive the merchants out of the temple." We have seen so many cases that are, in principle, just like this. In 1937 I came back from Tientsin to Chefoo and released a few messages there. In those messages I said that for us to follow the Lord we have to learn to bear the cross. I said that the mothers-in-law have to learn to bear the cross and that the daughters-in-law also have to learn to bear the cross. I also gave some examples from the Scriptures. After one of the meetings an elderly sister came to me and said, "Brother, your preaching was really from God. My daughter-in-law is very disobedient. The message that you released today was very much needed." The interesting thing is that after she had finished speaking and had left, another person came to me and said, "Brother, it is really hard to believe how badly the elderly sisters treat their daughters-in-law at home. You said that the mothers-in-law have to bear the cross. This is truly God's will." The message was the same, yet one person heard one thing while another person heard another thing. Likewise, the Bible is the same, yet one person reads one thing while another person reads another thing. We all have seen the condition of man, yet we have not seen the mystery of God. We know ethics, filial piety, propriety, justice, honesty, and the sense of shame, but we do not know the mystery of God. We think that as long as we behave ourselves in a certain way, we will be able to please God. Such a concept is of religion and is in blindness. The reason a person gropes in blindness is that he does not have revelation; he does not see. His inner being has not been enlightened so he has to grope in darkness. Although we are saved, I am afraid that even to this day we are still in religion. Have we really seen the revelation of God? The revelation of God is Christ. Only Christ is the purpose of God, and only Christ is the revelation of God. Only when a person has received such a revelation will he truly know the Christ of revelation and the service that is of revelation. Everything hinges on Christ. Whatever is not in Christ, no matter how beautiful it is, is of religion and not of God's revelation. Whatever is of God's revelation is Christ.

HAVING REVELATION, LIGHT, AND SIGHT

Revelation is like the lifting of a curtain, the opening of a veil. Yet once the veil is opened, there are two other requirements—light and sight. Even when the veil is lifted, if there is no light, we will not see. If there is light, but we do not have the sight, we still will not be able to see. In the New Testament age the revelation is already here, but the strangest thing is that many people still do not have the light or the vision in their reading of the Bible. Why is this? First, it is because they do not have light. Second, it is because they do not have the sight—their eyes are not opened. Before the veil is lifted, we surely will not see anything. But even after the veil is lifted, if there is no light, we still will not see anything. If our eyes are blind, even though there is light, we still will not see. But if our eyes are opened, we will be able to see the vision spoken of in the Scriptures. What is a vision? A vision is a scene, not an ordinary one, but a particular scene that we see from God.

Today when we come to the New Testament, all that is contained in the Bible has already been revealed. Yet when reading the Bible, if our eyes are not opened we will not be able to see the vision of God even though the word of God is right in front of us. But if our eyes are opened when we pray and read God's word, we will immediately see the vision. At that time the revelation will become our vision. While revelation is objective, vision is subjective. I hope that all of God's children will truly see something through this word and therefore put aside everything that is outward and traditional so that they can read God's Word carefully with a simple mind and a single eye. We should not read the Bible with our traditional concepts or with our colored eyeglasses. Rather, we should put aside all of our concepts and simply come to the Bible—the Word of God. If we do this, I believe that one day God will have mercy on us and show us His revelation. At that time we will know that God's mystery, God's treasure, and God's eternal purpose are just Christ. We look to God to save us in this matter so that we may see Christ. Only he who has seen Christ has seen the revelation, and only he who has seen the revelation can know God.

CHAPTER SEVEN

RELIGION OR REVELATION

All worship and service that is apart from Christ, though seemingly worship and service to God, is of religion. From the human perspective these things may seem to be very good, but they do not have much value in God's eyes. Serving in this way should be only an initial experience and should lead us to Christ. It is the most pitiful thing if one who serves God stays merely in religious practices. Any kind of religious service should be just an introductory experience that ushers us to Christ. From God's word we clearly see that only worship and service that are in Christ are of revelation. Any worship, any service that is apart from Christ is of religion.

THE MYSTERY OF GOD BEING CHRIST

From beginning to end God just wants us to have a relationship with Christ. We must know that God had a purpose in creating the universe and that for generations before the time of the apostles this purpose was never told to anyone. God hid this purpose in Himself and made it a mystery. According to Colossians 2:2, the mystery of God is Christ. God's purpose is Christ. God created the universe for His Son, Christ, and God redeemed us also for His Son, Christ. This is God's purpose, but until the time of the apostles He never told anyone; rather, this purpose was hidden in God Himself as a mystery. This hidden mystery of God is Christ.

GOD REVEALING THE MYSTERY TO THE APOSTLES

In the age of the apostles God opened the veil of the mystery to them (Eph. 3:3-5). Immediately, this unveiling became a revelation. God unveiled this mystery, which had been hidden throughout the ages, to the apostles and showed them that Christ is God's mystery, God's purpose. When this mystery was unfolded, what the apostles saw was Christ Himself. Hence, the revelation that the apostles saw was the revelation of Christ. Such a revelation was unveiled to the apostles. Previously, Christ was hidden; neither Abraham nor David nor any of the prophets in the Old Testament knew Him. Although Christ was spoken of in the Old Testament, those in the Old Testament did not know that this Christ is the center of the universe. It was not until the time of the apostles that God lifted the veil. Then the apostles were able to say that God's mystery is Christ. God does not want anything that is apart from Christ. Everything that is acceptable to God, praised by God, or counted by God is in Christ.

THE SERVICE THAT GOD DESIRES BEING CHRIST

Deep within me I have a feeling that I cannot utter. The apostle Paul wrote so many Epistles, yet there was only one central purpose—that the churches and the believers at that time would see that God's center is Christ. Anything that is outside of Christ, no matter how pious, good, or religious, is of no value in God's eyes. Paul said that although the Jews required signs and the Greeks sought wisdom, the apostles preached Christ crucified (1 Cor. 1:22-23). God did not want the apostles to preach signs or wisdom; instead, He wanted them to preach the crucified Christ as Lord. Why did He want this? It is because Christ is God's sign, God's wisdom, and God's power (v. 24). In the early church, some believers laid much emphasis on signs, and others very much stressed Greek wisdom. The apostles, however, told them that service before God is not a matter of signs or wisdom but a matter of Christ. Today the service that God desires is not related to signs or wisdom but is of Christ. What is of Christ is actually just Christ Himself.

ALL THE FULLNESS OF THE GODHEAD DWELLING IN CHRIST BODILY

Paul told the Galatians, "You observe days and months and seasons and years; I fear for you, lest I have labored upon you in vain" (Gal. 4:10-11). The Jews kept the law, practiced circumcision, and observed the feasts. Thus, Paul feared for them, lest his labor upon them be in vain. He said, "I travail again in birth until Christ is formed in you" (v. 19). It is not a matter of whether we keep the law, practice circumcision, or observe the feasts; rather, it is a matter of Christ. Has Christ been formed in us? This is the question of all questions. The churches in Galatia had a problem. They brought the service of Judaism and of religion into the church. Hence, Paul showed them that everything related to this kind of service was nothing. In the church there is room only for Christ. The problem with the Greeks was their wisdom. They allowed wisdom to enter into the church. The apostle showed them that their wisdom did not count for anything. Christ alone is everything.

Paul said, "In Him [Christ] dwells all the fullness of the Godhead bodily" (Col. 2:9). In other words, apart from Christ we cannot touch God, for God caused Himself to dwell in Christ bodily. Outside of Christ, neither philosophy, literature, nor even religion can enable us to touch or contact God because all the fullness of God Himself dwells in Christ bodily. The passages we have quoted from the Scriptures truly show us that the service that God desires is service that is in Christ. Anything that is outside of Christ, no matter how good or praiseworthy it is in man's eyes, is nothing and is of no value in God's eyes. We must see this principle.

"SALVATION" ACCORDING TO RELIGION

If we look at the practical experience of a person's salvation from a non-theological perspective, we can say that there are two kinds of salvation: the "salvation" of religion and the salvation of revelation. If a person experiences only the "salvation" according to religion but not salvation according to revelation, then basically he is not saved. A person's "salvation" is according to religion when it is mixed with religious things. Before a person believes in the Lord, he may not be concerned for his soul or think about religion. But after he is saved and begins to be concerned for his soul, his religious concepts come in. What is a religious concept? Some people think that after they are saved, they should repent thoroughly and be delivered from sins. In addition, they feel that from that point on they should look to God for mercy, depend on God's grace, be good people, never be cold or backsliding, and try their best to please God. In this way they consider that when they depart from the world and go to be with the Lord, the Lord will let them go to heaven seeing that they have had a thorough repentance and that their behavior was satisfactory. Do not think that I am too much to say this. This is the real situation. Many people think that after they are saved, they should wail for three days and three nights—rolling on the ground and shedding many tears—to wash away their sins so that when they see the Lord face to face, the Lord will consider them quite satisfactory, and they will be saved. Some people may not think exactly like this, but they think in a similar way. This is "salvation" according to religion, not salvation according to revelation.

SALVATION ACCORDING TO REVELATION

What then is salvation according to revelation? We may illustrate it in this way. One day after hearing a message, or while praying, reading the Bible, or even walking on the street, the Holy Spirit may mysteriously and inwardly show us that our Savior Christ was hanged on the cross to die for us and that He bore our sins in His body, resurrected from the dead, and released His life to us so that if we would receive such a Christ, our sins would be forgiven and we would receive His life within. As a result we exult, praise, and thank God, saying, "O God, I am a sinner, but You are holy. Thank You for dying for me. Within me there is darkness, but You are full of light. Thank You for Your life, for coming into me to be my life." Through this we are saved. This is salvation according to revelation.

However, the story is not that simple. According to revelation, some people are already saved, but according to the perspective of religion they are not yet saved. Perhaps you may wonder what this means. A person under the enlightening of the Holy Spirit may see that he needs a Savior and that the Lord Jesus is his Savior who shed His blood and bore his sins on the cross. As a result, he prays, "Thank You, Lord, I was full of sins, but You bore my sins on the cross. Thank You that though I am corrupted, evil, and in darkness, You are bright and holy, and You have become my life." A person is able to thank the Lord in such a way because he has seen the Christ who died and resurrected. But the strange thing is that after he prays, he may still say, "I am afraid that I may not be saved." If you would ask him why he says this, he may say, "I heard from someone that when he got saved, he cried and shed many tears so that all his sins were washed away. If I did not shed any tears, how can I be saved?" Then he may continue, "I also heard that when a person is saved, he should feel pricked in his heart and lament over his sins for three days and three nights. But I was not pricked in my heart, nor did I lament over my sins. Do you think that I am saved?" A while later he may also say, "When some people got saved, they prayed continuously until they saw a vision of the Lord Jesus hanging on the cross, shedding His blood for them. Then they wept and were saved. But I have never had these experiences. Am I really saved?" Thus, in terms of revelation such a person has been truly saved, but in terms of religion he has not.

Hence, from here we see that there are two experiences of "salvation": the experience that is according to revelation and the experience that is according to religion. The experience of "salvation" according to religion occurs when we have a set of concepts that are not the result of revelation and feel that as long as we do certain things, we will be accepted by God. An experience that is according to revelation occurs when the Holy Spirit removes the veil within us and reveals Christ in us, showing us that Christ died for us on the cross. Such an experience is a revelation. As children of God, we should know what it means to have something of religion and what it means to have something of revelation. When we were saved, did we first have revelation or religion? A genuine salvation is a salvation that comes out of revelation. When we see that Christ died for us on the cross and was resurrected for us, we are saved. After we are saved, we can begin to serve God.

SERVICE ACCORDING TO RELIGION

The same principle that we saw above applies to all of our Christian experiences. Every Christian experience can have two aspects: the aspect of religion and the aspect of revelation. Not only our experience of salvation may have these two aspects, but after we are saved, our service before God may also have these two aspects. We may ask, "What kind of living and service is according to religion, and what kind of living and service is according to revelation?" After we are saved, we may spontaneously have a concept that from that point on we need to be more zealous, to have more love, and to treat our wife better. In the same way, after we are revived, all these concepts may also come to us. Formerly, our living was loose and lukewarm, but now that we are saved and revived, we feel that we should be more serious and zealous. We also feel that we should preach the gospel, maintain a good testimony at home, love the brothers and sisters in the church, and always read the Bible and pray. All these concepts may come to us. Moreover, we may also bring these matters to God and pray, "O Lord, I was really bad in the past, but now that I am saved and revived, I need to be zealous and love the brothers and sisters. Yet I realize that I will not be able to do it persistently. Please have mercy on me, and help me every day so that I may be able to do it." Please remember that God listens to every kind of prayer except this kind of prayer.

When a wife who has a very bad temper and always argues with her husband at home gets saved and revived, the very first concept she has is that from that day on she should not argue with her husband or lose her temper with her children anymore. She realizes, however, that she is unreliable, so she brings this matter to God in prayer. Yet the fact is that God never listens to this kind of prayer. Even if she does make some changes, it will be because she was the one who listened to her prayer. She may not lose her temper on the first day because she is as careful as a person carrying a glass full of water. On the second day, however, she will not do as well as she did on the first day, but she still may not lose her temper.

Then on the third day she may ask God again to increase His keeping power so that she will not lose her temper. On the fourth day, however, she will probably lose her temper in a terrible way, even more terribly than she ever did before she prayed. After being revived many people have similar experiences. What is this? This is nothing but religion. We already have these concepts without having to touch God or read the Bible.

For example, suppose that one day a brother who treats his wife poorly is revived. Even though he does not pray, touch God, or touch Christ, he already has the concept that he should be kind to his wife. What kind of concept is this? Is it of revelation or of religion? It is a concept that comes from religion. Let me ask you again, after a person is saved or revived, if he spontaneously has the concept that he should be zealous without having been exhorted by others, is this something of religion or something of revelation? It is something of religion. Perhaps we all will be discouraged after we hear such a word. It seems that whatever we do is religious. Even our attempts to love our wife, be zealous, preach the gospel, and distribute tracts can all be something of religion. Then should we not try to do anything? Here is the problem. A person who does not do a certain thing cannot do it even if he wants to, and a person who does a certain thing cannot help doing it even if he does not want to do it anymore. For example, if someone does not love his wife, we may exhort him to love his wife. Yet regardless of how hard he tries, he simply cannot love his wife. However, after he is revived, if he genuinely touches Christ, it will be impossible for him not to love his wife even if we asked him not to.

SERVICE ACCORDING TO REVELATION

There is only one thing that we have that counts before God—Christ. We have to see at least once that Christ was crucified on the cross to bear our sins and that He is truly our Savior. We all must have this "one day" before we can say that we have been saved. We also must have a "one day" when the Holy Spirit shows us that it is no longer we but Christ. It is not we who submit to our husband, but it is Christ who submits. It is not we who love our wife, but it is Christ who loves. It is not we who are zealous, but it is Christ who is zealous. The Holy Spirit shows us that those who want to do good, who want to love their wives, and who want to submit to their husbands are already crucified with Christ, and now it is Christ who lives in them (Gal. 2:20). We are not the ones who do good, who are zealous, who love others, or who preach the gospel. We have been crucified with Christ, and now it is Christ who lives in us.

"ONE DAY"

We should have several "one days" in our lifetime. The first one should be when the Holy Spirit shows us that the Lord Jesus bore up our sins in His body and was resurrected from among the dead to be our life. This should be our first "one day." Then our second "one day" should be when we see that it was not merely the sinning "I" who was crucified on the cross but that even the "I" who does good was also crucified. It was not merely the "I" who has a bad temper who was crucified on the cross, but even the meek "I" was also crucified. The Holy Spirit shows us that we are already crucified with Christ and that it is no longer we who live, but Christ who lives in us. Galatians 2:20 says, "I am crucified with Christ; and it is no longer I who live, but it is Christ who lives in me." I have passed away, I am terminated, I am over, and I am already crucified. A living person can do evil and can also do good. But now that I have been put to death, can I still commit sin? No. Can this dead person still do good? No. Can a person who previously hit his wife but has now been crucified still hit his wife? No. Can he love his wife now? No. He is dead. He can neither hit his wife nor love his wife. This is to be a Christian.

A Christian is one who is dead both to sin and to good. A dead person can neither sin nor do good. "I am crucified with Christ; and it is no longer I who live, but it is Christ who lives in me." What does it mean to be a Christian? To be a Christian means that "it is no longer I who live, but it is Christ who lives in me." Because I am identified with Him, when He was crucified, I was also crucified. I was crucified with Him, and His death is my death. Such a death delivers me from my sins and my goodness. This is not a matter of doctrine but a matter of revelation.

Hence, we need another "one day" when the Holy Spirit shows us again that we are already crucified with Christ and that it is no longer we who live but Christ who lives in us. If we see this, we will no longer resolve to do good or be determined to do certain things; rather, we will simply praise. When we see this and praise Him for this, Christ will have more ground in us and will be expressed through us. When Christ is magnified in us, we will love our wife, submit to our husband, and love sinners. However, the love and submission will not be our doing but the overflow of Christ. We have already been crucified. When Christ gains the ground in us, He will be expressed through us. At that time, we will really love our wife, submit to our husband, be zealous, and have the love for sinners. However, we will not be conscious of how much we have done. Rather, we will only have the sense that we are crucified with Christ and that He is living in us. This is service according to revelation.

Hence, when we see Christ for the first time in our Christian life and in our Christian path, we see that He was crucified and died for us and that we are saved. Eventually we will also see that when Christ died for us on the cross to save us, we ourselves were also crucified. When we see this, we will not do anything because a dead person can neither do good nor have any hope. We will see that we are finished. We will see that it is no longer we who live but that it is Christ who lives in us. At this time we will see that once we go out, He comes in. From that day onward, we simply will not be able to make any resolutions or to have any hope in ourselves, because we will realize that it is no longer we who live, but Christ who lives in us. At this moment our Christian life truly begins.

Although we may be saved, if we do not know this way, we will still live within the realm of religion. This will be the case until one day the Holy Spirit will show us that we are crucified. Then we will be truly terminated in our experience. From that day onward it will be no longer we who serve but Christ who serves. Our Christian living will not really begin until that day.

CHAPTER EIGHT

SERVICE ACCORDING TO RELIGION
OR
SERVICE ACCORDING TO REVELATION

SERVING IN THE SPIRIT OF GOD

In Philippians 3:3, Paul said, "For we are the circumcision, the ones who serve by the Spirit of God and boast in Christ Jesus and have no confidence in the flesh." Here the apostle referred to service that is by the Spirit of God. According to the Greek, serve by the Spirit of God may also be translated as *serve in the Spirit of God*. This kind of service in the Spirit of God is service in Christ Jesus. Therefore, this verse also tells us that those who serve by the Spirit of God boast in Christ Jesus and not in the flesh. The first half of verse 7 reads, "But what things were gains to me." From the context we know that the things that Paul referred to as gains to him were the items related to religion, because the items he criticized in the preceding verses were the items of religion. He was a real Jew, circumcised on the eighth day. He was also very zealous and was blameless according to the law. All these things pertained to the Jewish religion. Formerly he considered these things gain to him, but now he counted them as loss on account of Christ.

SERVICE ACCORDING TO RELIGION

Concerning the matter of service, there is service according to religion, and there is also service according to revelation. What is service that is according to religion? Any service that is not in Christ, whether it is service that comes out of our natural being or service that comes from tradition, is service according to religion. Apart from Christ, we may have many thoughts and concepts that are evil, filthy, sinful, and against God. This is the bad side. However, there is also a good side that is apart from Christ. We may also have some good concepts. We may think about worshipping God and seeking after God, and we may also think about using different ways to serve God. This is the good side of our natural man. This good side includes things related to serving God and things related to human conduct. Serving God and human conduct constitute the two aspects of religion. To practice religion is to have certain beliefs related to these two aspects and to teach according to these beliefs. Hence, religion stresses worshipping God and teachings related to human conduct.

Religion is in man. If a person commits sin or does evil, he will not want to worship God. This is the evil side of the natural man. Nevertheless, the natural man also has a good side. When a person has the desire to do good, he spontaneously thinks about God and wants to worship and serve God. Since man has this thought regarding serving and worshipping God, he will automatically consider his living and think that he should conduct himself properly and do things well. All of this is religion. This is what we mean by service that is according to religion.

In terms of human conduct religion is good, admirable, and honorable, but in terms of God's salvation and God's revelation, even all these good things have to be put aside. They are hindrances to God's salvation and opponents to God's revelation. This matter is quite mysterious. If a person has no thought of God at all, that is, if he has no thought of religion at all, we will have no way to lead him to know God and worship God. In like manner, we cannot help a chicken or an ox to know God because they do not have the thought, the natural ability, or even the inclination to know God. They have no ideas about God and are not interested in God. When a person is living in sin, he may not have any interest in God. Yet when he feels miserable and depressed due to a certain situation, he will become interested in God because there is the thought of religion in him. It is because of this concept of religion that we are able to preach the gospel and lead people to know God. We can lead someone to God only when he has such a concept of religion. The mysterious thing is that a person must have this concept of religion for him to know God, but according to the Scriptures once he touches and knows God, he needs to put this concept of religion aside. Otherwise, this concept of religion will become a hindrance to his enjoyment of God's salvation.

PUTTING ASIDE THE CONCEPT OF RELIGION AFTER SALVATION

To put aside the concept of religion after salvation is just like "destroying the bridge after having crossed the river," as the Chinese people say. Without the bridge there is no way to cross the river, but after we have crossed the river, we have to destroy the bridge immediately. Without the concept of religion we have no way to come to God and to know God. If we hold on to our religious concepts, however, we have no way to know God in a further way. Hence, please remember that immediately after we receive the Lord and once we possess God, we must drop our religious concepts. Otherwise, these concepts will become a big problem in our Christian life. It is not because of sin or the world that many people do not have much growth in life and cannot have further knowledge of God after their salvation. The biggest problem lies with the religious concepts within them. A saved one may think that since he sinned and did evil in the past, now that he is saved and has become a child of God, he should practice doing good. This is in accordance with his concept of religion. He thinks that although this concept of doing good was formerly obliterated by his sins and evil doings, now that he is saved and has come to the church, he will surely have the opportunity for this concept to be put to use. Therefore, he instinctively applies his concepts of religion—serving God, being zealous, conducting himself as a man, doing good, behaving himself, being meek and obedient—to all aspects of his Christian life.

These concepts, which are one hundred percent religious, are not derived from God's enlightenment or teaching that a person may receive after he has been saved. Actually, these concepts were in him long before he was saved. Thus, now that he is saved, he brings these religious concepts into the church. On the one hand, he has the concept that he must serve God; on the other hand, he has the concept that he has to conduct himself properly as a man. If he does well in these two aspects, he considers himself a perfect man. He never searches the Bible to find out what a standard Christian is. He has only ethical and religious concepts, which are all natural and traditional and do not require the enlightenment and confirmation of the Holy Spirit. Later, this will become a big hindrance and an opponent to God in his experience. May God be merciful to us and open our eyes to show us that the kind of service He desires is totally different from the kind of service we imagine according to our original religious concepts. If God is merciful to us to show us such a difference, we will surely put aside whatever we had before, whether it be sinful or ethical. Before we received revelation, owing to a lack of light, we thought that what was acceptable to God and profitable to us was something moral and religious. Now that we have been enlightened by God, however, we see that the service that God desires is not something religious but is in another realm.

TWO KINDS OF SERVICE

What we have said above is based on Philippians 3, in which chapter we see two kinds of service. One is service in spirit, service that is in Christ; the other is service in the flesh, service that is outside of Christ. Although both of them aim at service and worship to God, they are in different realms, on different grounds, from different sources, and have different natures. I hope that we who have a heart for God and a desire to serve God will see that Philippians 3 plainly speaks of these two kinds of service. Paul's is an example of one who had these two kinds of service. Previously, he served God in religion—he was circumcised, he was zealous, and he did his best to keep all the commandments of the law. In other words, he tried to serve God on the one hand and to conduct himself properly as a man on the other. Toward God, he was exceedingly zealous; before man, he kept the law of God diligently. He could be considered a blameless person and a good pattern for followers of religion. The religious followers of Christianity today are far inferior to the way Paul was in his time. Nevertheless, Paul said that his service was apart from Christ, apart from the Holy Spirit. Hence, this kind of service is religious. Such service is not in Christ or in the Spirit but is outside of the Spirit. This kind of service requires confidence in the flesh but not in the Spirit. Therefore, these two kinds of service come from two different sources and have two different natures. One is in the Spirit whereas the other is in the flesh. One has confidence in the Spirit whereas the other has confidence in the flesh. One cannot do anything without the Spirit whereas the other can do everything without the Spirit. The latter is the service in religion while the former is the service in Christ. Paul suffered the loss of all things of religion that he might gain Christ.

RELIGIOUS SERVICE REPLACING CHRIST

Religious service is a replacement of Christ. If we have religious service, we do not have Christ because religious service replaces Christ. We can also say that religion usurps the position of Christ and opposes Christ. For this reason, and in order to gain Christ, Paul suffered the loss of his religious service. This was absolutely right. Whenever religious service gains the ground in a person, it will be difficult for that person to know Christ in a deeper way. The problem that hinders a person the most from growing in life properly and knowing Christ thoroughly after his salvation is having too many religious concepts. Religious concepts fill and occupy a person so that Christ has no ground in him and has no way to express Himself through him. If a person is filled with so many religious things, including religious thoughts, concepts, and inclinations, he has no way to know more of Christ and of God.

RELIGIOUS CONCEPTS BEING
A PROBLEM TO CHRISTIANS

May we all see that religious concepts are a problem. We think that sins, the world, the flesh, and the devil are the only problems facing a Christian. We may think that as long as we have thoroughly dealt with these four things—sins, the world, the flesh, and the devil—we will be able to be perfect Christians. Please do not forget that this kind of Christian is most likely one who lives merely by his religious concepts. This kind of person probably has never been enlightened or seen the revelation. All he has is ordinary religious concepts. However, once he receives the shining of God, he will see that the most subjective problem facing Christians is not sins, the world, the flesh, or the devil, but the religious concept of doing good that is within them.

RELIGIOUS CONCEPTS BELONGING TO THE TREE OF THE KNOWLEDGE OF GOOD AND EVIL AND THE ISSUE OF CONTACTING THIS TREE BEING DEATH

In the Old Testament we see that God put man in the garden of Eden. In this garden there were two trees—one was the tree of the knowledge of good and evil, and the other was the tree of life (Gen. 2:9). There was no third tree. The tree of life, no doubt, was for man to receive life. What was the tree of the knowledge of good and evil? The Bible says, "For in the day that you eat of it you shall surely die" (v. 17). From this we see that the tree of the knowledge of good and evil was not meant to be touched. Whoever contacted it would die. The tree of the knowledge of good and evil had both good and evil. God said that the issue of contacting the tree of the knowledge of good and evil would be death. The issue of contacting evil is death, and the issue of contacting good is also death. Only life is life and will be forever life. Good is not life and cannot replace life. Anything that is apart from life, whether it is good or evil, is not life. Only life is life. Anything that is outside of life is not life. Hence, even though religious and ethical concepts may be good, they are apart from life and cannot touch life.

This does not mean that we should not do good, perform good deeds, or have any religious concepts. Although religious concepts may be good, they serve only as a bridge to lead man to Christ. Once we have been led to Christ, however, we should not treasure the bridge; rather, we should destroy it. If we do not destroy it, there may be a chance that we would go back. Thus, some Christians are advancing and then retreating all the time. After a person has been led to God by his religious concepts, he should immediately condemn and destroy that concept. "What things were gains" to him should be "counted as loss" once he knows and sees Christ as the One of peerless worth in the universe (Phil. 3:7-8). If he treasures his religious concept and his religious service, he will have no way to enjoy more of Christ. A person may be truly saved yet still have a very superficial experience of Christ and no spiritual progress at all. This is because he is full of religious concepts. Since he is still living by his religious concepts, he has no way to know Christ in a deeper way. This problem is altogether due to the religious concepts within him.

THE DIFFERENCE BETWEEN
REVELATION AND RELIGION

We already know what is meant by service according to religion, but do we understand what service according to revelation is? Service according to revelation is service that is according to the revealed Christ. Any service that we do without touching Christ or contacting Christ is not service according to revelation; rather, it is religious service. Only when we contact Christ can our service be according to revelation. This is the same with our salvation. Only salvation that is according to revelation counts. What is salvation according to revelation? It is the salvation in which a person touches and contacts Christ. "Salvation" according to religion follows a formula. As long as a person fulfills a first, second, and third step, and as long as he carries out a certain procedure, he is considered saved. This is the "salvation" according to religion, which "salvation" does not count before God. The salvation that counts before God does not require man to do a first, second, and third step. Our salvation before God has no formula. When we touch Christ in our spirit, we are saved before God. This is salvation according to revelation.

This is not the case only with our service and salvation. All of our Christian experiences are the same. For example, what is holiness according to revelation in the Scriptures?

And what is holiness according to a formula? Holiness according to a formula is something of religion, not of revelation. One day God opens our eyes and shows us that Christ is not only our Savior and our life but the One who lives in us and who is our holiness. This is holiness according to revelation. Everything that is according to revelation has Christ. Everything that is according to religion does not have Christ.

CHRIST BEING OUR PATIENCE

In 1933 in Shanghai, I met Brother Watchman Nee, who was a very deep brother in the Lord. One day he asked me, "Brother, what is patience?" I thought that this should be an easy question to answer, but because of Brother Nee's depth in the Lord I also thought that it must not be that simple, so I dared not answer. He asked me again, "What is patience?" Then I said, "When we endure others' persecution by gritting our teeth, is this not patience?" He said, "Brother, this is not patience." Then I turned the question back to him, and he said, "Patience is Christ." Later, I thought about this over and over again, considering how patience could be Christ. Thank God! It was because of this word that I came to know God in a deeper way. On that day God opened my eyes to see what patience is.

Religious patience is patience that requires great endurance. For example, when my wife troubles me, I restrain my temper and say nothing; likewise, when your husband gives you hardship, you do not react. This is what we consider patience. However, this kind of patience is artificial and is of the flesh. It does not require man to be in the Spirit or in Christ. It is altogether based on man's own effort. If we have this kind of patience, we will have confidence in our flesh and will boast in our own ability to endure. Yet this is not what God desires. Such religious patience is artificial and is apart from Christ. One day God will show us that He does not want this kind of patience because it results in giving glory to man. God will show us that the glorious Christ who lives in us is our patience. When our wife troubles us, we do not need to try to restrain our temper and keep quiet. When our husband distresses us, we do not need to try to exercise our magnanimity or be extraordinarily patient, because Christ is in us bearing everything and living in us to be our patience. This is something apart from man's work, something in Christ. This is not our own patience but is the living out of Christ.

THE CONTENT OF THE BIBLE BEING CHRIST

We all know that Christians take the Bible as the basis of their living and work. But what does the Bible really speak about? A chemistry book talks about chemistry, and a mathematics book talks about mathematics. The Bible, however, speaks concerning Christ. If we take Christ away from the Bible, there will be nothing left but skin and feathers without any content, because the Bible is a portrait of Christ. In John 1 Christ is called the Word of God. The Greek word for *Word* is *logos*. Christ is the living Word of God, and the Bible is the written word of God. The written word is a portrayal of the living Word. Hence, the content of the Bible is Christ.

Since the Bible is focused on Christ, if we see only patience but do not see Christ in our reading of the Bible, there is a problem with our reading. Why is it that when a person reads the Bible—a book on Christ—he cannot see Christ but can see only patience, humility, and meekness? The reason is that he has not dropped his religious concepts. Many people are filled in their religious mind with humility, meekness, and patience. Even before they read the Bible, all these things are already in them. Hence, when they read the Bible, they find that the Bible also talks about humility, meekness, and patience. This exactly matches the things in their religious mind. Hence, greatly astonished, they consider the Bible to be a wonderful book. Little do they know that the Bible says that if there is any encouragement, it is *in Christ,* and if there is any consolation, it is *in Christ* (Phil. 2:1). The crucial phrase is *in Christ,* yet it seems that Bible readers have not seen it.

CHRIST BEING EVERYTHING

The love referred to in the Bible is the love in Christ, the love in the Holy Spirit. The virtues mentioned in the Bible are all in Christ. When people come to read the Bible, however, all they see are the virtues it describes, such as patience, love, and humility; they miss Christ altogether. How can this be? This is because the thought of being "in Christ" does not exist in the human mind. Hence, it is not easy for us to see this. Therefore, I hope that we will disdain the concepts in our mind instead of regarding them highly. If we are willing to condemn and drop our religious concepts, then when we read the Bible, we will see that the most central and precious matter in the Bible is Christ Himself. Instead of merely seeing some fragmented teachings, we will see the revelation that Christ is all and in all (Col. 3:11). Without Christ, there are no virtues. Without Christ, there is no love, no patience, and no humility. Without Christ, there is no spiritual reality. With Him, there is everything. He is everything, and He is the content of the Bible.

Moreover, we can also say that we have the Bible without and the Spirit within. The Bible without portrays Christ, and the Spirit within reveals Christ. Regrettably, however, today many saved ones have the Spirit within them, but the Spirit has no ground in them and has no opportunity to reveal Christ to them. Why? Because they are full of religious concepts. Since they are filled with religious concepts, the Holy Spirit does not have any opportunity or ground to speak, to enlighten, or to reveal Christ to them. If they see that all religious things are replacements and enemies of Christ and are willing to condemn all of these religious concepts, the Holy Spirit will have the opportunity and ground to reveal Christ to them day by day. In brief, we cannot see the revelation of Christ when we read the Bible because we have religious concepts within us. The Holy Spirit is also unable to reveal Christ to us due to our religious concepts. Hence, we have to condemn our religious concepts. Like Paul, we have to suffer the loss of all these things and count them as refuse that we may gain Christ (Phil. 3:7-8).

Chapter Nine

CONCERNING THE CHURCH

I am afraid that many people are not clear about the difference between the church and the various Christian organizations. The matter of the church is an exceedingly great matter. Let us take a look at this matter in the Scriptures.

There is a clear exposition of the church in the New Testament. The New Testament not only plainly records the matter of the church but also clearly sets before us the pattern of the church. Hence, many Bible readers acknowledge that the Bible is more than clear in its speaking concerning the church. God not only explained the church in plain words but also drew a picture. It can be said that He has given us a well-illustrated text. Therefore, there should not be any ambiguity concerning the church.

THERE BEING ONLY ONE BODY

The Bible shows us with clear words that there is only one church, which is the Body of Christ (Eph. 1:22b-23) and that Christ is the Head of the church (Col. 1:18). It is impossible for a head to have several bodies. A head can have only one body. Although the church is composed of many people, there is only one church throughout the ages and in all places because Christ has only one Body. The utterance in the Bible concerning the church as the Body defines the church quite accurately. If we said that the church was a garment, it would be possible for there to be more than one garment. You and I may not have the same number of garments, yet we both have only one body. There are many "ones" mentioned in the Bible. For example, there is only *one* God, *one* Lord, and *one* faith

(Eph. 4:5-6), and we drink *one* Spirit (1 Cor. 12:13). These "ones" all relate to the church. Whenever the church is mentioned, it is a matter of being one. The church is one. If we are to speak about the church, we must see this oneness. Moreover, it is not simply a matter of being united but a matter of being one. The church is one, just as our body is one. Since the church is one, the Bible shows us that the last prayer of the Lord Jesus on the earth was to ask God to keep His disciples so that they would be one on the earth (John 17:11, 21-22). Once the Body was produced, it was one. We need to keep such a oneness and not divide it. In the church in Corinth, however, we see that the flesh came out. Some people said that they were of Apollos—they considered him to be a competent preacher of the Scriptures. Others said that they were of Peter—they considered him to be the number one apostle. On the day of Pentecost he stood up to give a testimony, and three thousand people were saved. Peter also opened the door for the Gentiles. Still others said that they were of Paul—these ones had not been saved through Apollos or through Peter. Furthermore, there were those who said that they were of Christ—they followed no one but Christ and considered that all the others were wrong because they were of the flesh and of men. In the book of 1 Corinthians *of* is mentioned four times: *of* Paul, *of* Apollos, *of* Peter, and *of* Christ. The oneness of the Body of Christ—the church—was damaged by these four "of's" (1 Cor. 1:10-13). Therefore, Paul wrote the Corinthians a stern letter to rebuke them.

THE EXPRESSION OF THE CHURCH
TAKING THE LOCALITY AS THE BOUNDARY

On the one hand, the Bible shows us that the church is universally one; on the other hand, it shows us that the church is expressed in many localities. For example, there were the seven churches in Asia: the church in Ephesus, the church in Smyrna, the church in Pergamos, the church in Thyatira, the church in Sardis, the church in Philadelphia, and the church in Laodicea (Rev. 1:4, 11). The church was expressed in each of these cities. In the age of the apostles there was an expression in Jerusalem (Acts 8:1), in Antioch (13:1), and in Corinth

(1 Cor. 1:2). Now all over the world there are thousands of expressions of the church, including one in Taipei, one in New York, and one in London. Although there are thousands of expressions locally, the church itself is still one universally.

The expression of the church takes the locality as its boundary. History shows us that at the beginning of the church the population of Jerusalem may have been around one million. Even though the population was great, the Bible shows us that there was only one church in Jerusalem. On one day three thousand were saved and on another day five thousand were saved, but they still belonged to the church in Jerusalem. This is because the expression of the church takes the locality as its boundary. How great the boundary of a certain locality is determines how great the boundary of the church in that locality is. Likewise, how small the boundary of a locality is determines how small the boundary of the church in that locality is. In Lystra (Acts 14:6, 21), a small city whose population was probably no more than twenty to thirty thousand, there was only one church. The church itself is universal while its expression is local. The boundary of a local expression should be the jurisdiction of the locality at that time. There are churches that are in cities as big as a county, churches that are in cities that serve as capitals, and churches in cities the size of towns or villages. However, there are no churches on a particular street. There is no such thing as the church on Hoping Road or the church on Ren-ai Road. The Bible has only local churches. There is only one church universally, but there are thousands of local expressions. The only separation that may be allowed among the churches is separation by locality. Within a locality, however, there should not be any separation. If there is a separation, it is a division. This is the truth of the Bible.

THE PRACTICAL SITUATION OF THE CHURCH

The actual situation of the church, however, is not this way. It is full of divisions. All God's children seemingly have some knowledge of God, of God's grace, and of God's mercy, yet most do not have any knowledge concerning the church. If they really knew the church, they would not dare to be divided. Much confusion is caused because men are too bold, do not have adequate light, and live in darkness. If their eyes were enlightened by God, they would not be so careless. However, today God's children are seriously divided. They are not only divided, but they also have much mixture in their divisions. Therefore, the matter of the church is really a problem among Christians today.

A PURE HEART BEING REQUIRED
FOR US TO SERVE GOD

Once we rise up to serve God, God will require something of us. The Bible shows us that if God's children rise up to serve God while the church is in a desolate and divided situation, God's first requirement is that they should be pure in heart. Second Timothy 2:17-22 says, "And their word will spread like gangrene...who concerning the truth have misaimed, saying that the resurrection has already taken place....But flee youthful lusts, and pursue righteousness, faith, love, peace with those who call on the Lord out of a pure heart." The first half of this passage tells us that the church at that time was in such a state of confusion that some people even said that the resurrection had already taken place. Hence, Paul charged Timothy to be delivered and set apart from this confusion in order to be a vessel unto honor. He also asked Timothy to pursue righteousness, faith, love, and peace with those who called on the Lord out of a pure heart. In the midst of an age of confusion, if a person wants to serve God, he has to be pure in heart. What does it mean to be pure in heart? Matthew 5:8 says, "Blessed are the pure in heart, for they shall see God." If we put these few verses together, we will see that to be pure in heart means to desire nothing other than God Himself. Only the pure in heart can take the way of the church.

The intrinsic cause of today's sects and denominations is the inward impurity of man. To be impure does not mean that a person has some inward sins; rather, it means that he is seeking after something other than God. This means that this person's heart is not pure enough. For example, someone may say, "We can meet anywhere. Why do you say that we have to meet here?" The fact that a person says such a thing proves that his heart is not pure, because such a one has a desire and preference other than God. If he desires God alone, he will say, "O God, I come to meet in this place because of the pure ground, not because of any person. The fact that I come here has nothing to do with any person. I take this way because I simply want You. I only want You." This is to be pure in heart.

Suppose there is a person who puts the proper ground of God aside. He chooses to meet in a certain place only if the responsible brothers there act humbly toward him. Where do you think this person's heart is? If a person simply wants God, he will not care what kind of treatment he receives. We come to the meetings not for other things but only to touch God. Some people have said that they come to the meetings because our preaching is good. May I ask then, "If we did not have good preaching, would you still come?" Once a woman is married, her husband becomes her ground, and she must stay in her husband's home. If she leaves her husband's home and switches to another home because she does not eat well in her husband's home, she will be an adulteress. I hope that we all would see that in the midst of the desolation and confusion of the church today, only a group of people who are pure in heart will be able to find the way of the church and the ground of the church.

There are few among God's children today who know the ground of the church. Some people are very happy when the responsible brothers frequently greet them. When this happens, they immediately feel that this church is good and decide that they will come more often. But if the responsible brothers do not greet them one day, they will not come to the meetings anymore and will even go and meet in another place. It is all right for a housemaid to work in different homes, but it is not all right for a wife to be a wife in different homes. Mrs. Liu cannot say that because her husband is not nice to her, she has to go to the Chang family. We all have to be absolute, and we all must be able to tell God, "O God, today I take this way not for any other reason but because I am clear about this way." When a wife is married to someone, her husband's home becomes her stand. Whether he is poor or rich, proud or humble, she remains in his home. She cannot change her stand just because something about him changes.

DESIRING NOTHING BUT GOD HIMSELF

While on the path of our Christian life we have received the Lord's mercy to see the ground of the church. Thus, we have to tell Him, "Lord, I want nothing but You." Today if we desire something other than God, we will not be able to find the way of the church, and we will immediately lose the ground of the church. Some people meet at a certain place because they are able to preach the gospel there. However, if they are not able to preach the gospel, they will leave right away. Instead of loving God, these people love the evangelistic work. Therefore, they stay at a certain place, not for God or anything else, but for the evangelistic activities. All problems arise because our heart is not pure, and we desire something other than God. If we are those who simply desire God, we will see that the church is universally one and that its local expression should also be one. Everything else is mixed with human opinion and intentions. This is not what God desires, and this needs to be condemned.

SERVING GOD ON THE GROUND OF LOCALITY

If there is a group of brothers in Tainan who stand on this pure ground to serve God, and they make a declaration before the universe—"O God, we are simply Your children. We do not belong to any denomination or sect but only to You. We serve You on the ground of locality"—this will be a testimony to the world that they are not any kind of denomination, but they are a group of Christians who desire God alone and who want only to serve God on the ground of locality. If this were to happen, I believe that all those who have a pure heart would be drawn and would be enlightened to acknowledge such a ground.

If a brother who is not from Tainan moves to Tainan, and there is already a local church with some responsible ones in Tainan, what should this brother do? Do not think that all Christians are holy. Just as there are many who compete for high places in the political arena, so there are also some who vie for high positions in the church. Instead of joining the existing church, this brother may consider starting another one. The ground of the local church is already there in Tainan, and those who are in the church are truly Christians who are pure in heart and who serve God with a pure heart. Thus, he cannot find any fault with them. Therefore, he has no choice but to join them if he wants to serve God in Tainan. After much consideration, however, he may not be sure as to whether they will let him preach the word. So he goes to God and prays, "O God, should I join them, or should I establish another 'church,' a congregational church?" The more he prays, the more he feels that God wants him to set up a congregational church. Then, at that very moment a zealous Christian tells him that there is a piece of land available for his use. Therefore, he is even more full of thanks and praises to God for His provision. Thus, after starting a new congregational church, he preaches from the podium, saying, "We are the such-and-such chapel, and we are non-denominational." He may claim to be non-denominational, but his speaking is actually divisive. The Bible tells us that in the church there cannot be Greek and Jew (Col. 3:11). The church cannot be divided into "chapels." If someone establishes a "chapel," it is a terrible sect and a human invention. There is no such thing in the Bible.

If our heart is not pure, sooner or later we will initiate something that does not correspond with what the Bible says. Someone once asked why is it that we do not cooperate with the various Christian organizations. Actually, which one among them is really cooperating with the others? Among the denominations in Christianity, which one of them does not have its own name? One of them operates the Bread of Life Church, another one manages the Chinese Evangelistic Mission, a third one operates the Salvation Army, and a fourth one manages the Fellowship Alliance. Every preacher, as long as he has a certain degree of fame, has a congregation under his own management. This is the case not only in Mainland China, but even in Taiwan today it is impossible for two famous preachers to labor together. By the Lord's grace, however, although some among us who are laboring for the

Lord in various places are very gifted, they are still able to labor together with others instead of doing a particular work of their own. This is because our eyes have been enlightened by God, causing us to fear God and to realize our own limitation.

While taking the Lord's way of the church, we should not have any personal relationships or personal affection. I once told Brother Watchman Nee, who rendered me much help, "Even if one day you would not take this way, I will still take it." May we all be able to say that even if all the leading brothers among us fall and forsake the Lord, we still will take this way. Our taking this way has nothing to do with man; rather, it is by the Lord's mercy and grace. If we see this, we will pay attention to the church and to the ground of the church. Regardless of how divisive other people may be, we ourselves would not be divisive.

Furthermore, I hope that we are all clear about why we need such a ground. Although there are many local expressions of the church, there is only one expression in each locality. The church is one universally and it is also one locally. Suppose we are serving the Lord in Tainan, but one day the Lord brings us to Hualien where some brothers are meeting who do not belong to any denomination and who simply serve the Lord purely. When we arrive there, we should join them and meet with them. We should see that when we were in Tainan, we were brothers in Tainan, but now that we have come to Hualien, we are brothers in Hualien. This is the proper ground.

NEEDING THE AUTHORITY OF THE HOLY SPIRIT
IN ADDITION TO THE PROPER GROUND

Nevertheless, we should not think that once we have the proper ground everything is all right. It is one thing to have the proper ground, but it is another thing to have the authority of the Holy Spirit. In addition to standing on the proper ground, we also need to allow the Holy Spirit to exercise His authority among us. One necessity is a matter of the ground, and the other is a matter of the authority of the Holy Spirit. Even if we have the proper ground here in Taipei, if the Holy

Spirit does not have authority among us, the condition here will surely be improper. Suppose you have the proper ground in Pingtung, but you do not allow the Holy Spirit to have the authority. If this is the case, your situation will also be bad. This requires our flesh to be dealt with by the cross of Christ. This kind of dealing will allow the Holy Spirit to have the authority in the church. All God's children have to learn to give God the authority. You should never say, "We are the responsible brothers in the church, so the authority is in our hands." Every one of us has to learn to accept the dealing of the cross because there is no place for the flesh in the church.

Every time we meet together we have to hang ourselves on the cross. Otherwise, the Holy Spirit will not have the authority in the church. Instead, the flesh will reign instead of the Holy Spirit. If our flesh has been dealt with, we will be like those in Acts 15. Even though there was much discussion among them, they did not quarrel. The saints will be able to sit down together and have a discussion only if their flesh has been dealt with. Otherwise, they will quarrel as soon as they begin their discussion. Even though they may have different views, the responsible brothers can discuss something for several hours without quarreling, because their flesh has been dealt with. For the Holy Spirit to have the authority in the church, there must be the proper ground and the proper condition of the church. One requirement is the ground, and the other is the proper condition.

JUDGING A CHURCH
NOT ACCORDING TO ITS CONDITION
BUT ACCORDING TO ITS GROUND

Nevertheless, we should not judge a church according to its condition, but according to its ground. One time I met a believer in Manila. He told me that he could not come to the meetings because he did not agree with the practice of a certain brother in the church. This is wrong. Regardless of whether or not the practice of a particular brother is correct, his condition has nothing to do with the ground of the church.

If we want to find out whether or not a church is of God and whether or not we should join it, we should make our judgment according to the ground of the church and not according to the condition of the church. After a man is married, his wife may find several faults in him and want to divorce him, but can a wife decide whether or not her husband's home is her home according to the present condition of her husband? Can she say that because her husband is not proper, his home is not her home? She cannot say this. We cannot judge whether or not a church is of God based on the condition of the responsible brothers. For example, when your temper is good, your wife acknowledges that your home is her home, and when you lose your temper, she still has to admit that your home is her home. We cannot say that because the responsible brothers in a certain place are more spiritual, the church there is of God; neither can we say that because the responsible brothers there are too fleshly, the church there is not of God. We can only say that because the responsible brothers are fleshly, the Holy Spirit does not have the authority there. Hence, the ground of the church is one thing, and the condition of the church is another. The ground is local, and upon the ground of locality the church should allow the Holy Spirit to have the authority.

A church should have a good condition as well as the proper ground. If a church does not have any outward signboard but inwardly has the authority of the Holy Spirit, this is the best. Some among the seven churches in Revelation were in a poor condition. Although they were in an improper condition, the Lord still addressed them as churches. From this we see that we should judge a church not according to its condition but according to its ground.

QUESTIONS AND ANSWERS CONCERNING THE CHURCH

The Church Being a Great Test

Someone once asked what we should do if two churches with similar conditions but different grounds were established in the same locality on the same day by two different persons? This question is one hundred percent based on a supposition, and it would be very hard for such a thing to happen. In fact, it would be impossible for two churches to have the same condition and begin their meeting on the same day. If a meeting has already been raised up in a locality on the clear and proper ground, we should simply join the believers there when we go there. How could we raise up another church? If a woman has been married, no one else can take her and marry her. If she is married again, this will be bigamy. If there is no clear and proper ground in a certain locality, we have the ground to start to meet there. However, if there is already the clear and proper ground, and we establish another meeting, this will be a denomination. This violates the principle of taking the locality as the boundary.

If two meetings of similar condition were raised up at different times in the same locality, in order to decide which one has the proper ground, we would have to look at when they were established. Moreover, we could also inquire into their genealogy. In the Bible there is such a thing as inquiring into one's genealogy. In the Old Testament a group of priests were excluded from the service of God because their names were not found in the genealogical registry of Israel (Neh. 7:61-65).

Only those whose eyes have been enlightened will make inquiries concerning the matter of the church. The majority of people simply do not care. Some people may ask, "Isn't it good that some have a desire to serve God? Isn't it good that some sisters who previously did not practice head covering have been covering their heads since they began meeting with us?" We have to remember that God does not take the matter of the church lightly. Rather, God is very serious and will not approve of anything ambiguous. Nothing tests us more than the church. Once we touch this matter, our inward condition is exposed. When we talk about prayer, our problems are not that exposed. When we talk about gospel preaching, our problems are not that exposed. When we talk about pursuing the Lord, our problems are not that exposed. However, once we talk about the matter of the church, our inner condition is completely exposed. Once we touch the matter of the church, we are put to the test. Over these past years we have learned to base eighty percent of our knowledge concerning a person upon how he views the church.

For example, recently someone said, "How good it is to have believers and the Lord's gospel everywhere!" This word sounds nice and is pleasant to one's ears. But the fact is that not only is such a person ignorant regarding the church, but he is also indifferent. He has never learned any basic or serious lessons before God. Only those who have not learned any serious lessons before God could say that this situation is good. Those who have learned serious lessons would never say that this is good, because they know what is good and what is not good. A person who has genuine insight and has learned some lessons before God would not consider that the situation everywhere is the same.

Having the Universal Fellowship
on the Ground of Locality

Someone once asked, "It is said that there is a group of people meeting in Kangshan whose condition is similar to ours and who also do not have a name for themselves. What kind of attitude should we have toward them?" We need to be clear concerning the basic matter of the church. On the one hand, the church is expressed locally, and on the other hand, the church is universal. Do not think that since we are the church in Pingtung, we do not need to care about other Christians in the world or that it is good enough just to meet as the church in Pingtung. If some Christians are raised up in Kangshan who are also on the clear and proper ground but do not have any contact with other churches, then they will soon become a denomination. When we see the seriousness of this, we will know how to render help to them. We should not condemn them or put any demand on them; rather, we should have much fellowship with them. Then at a certain stage in the fellowship they will be enlightened inwardly. They will see that their being raised up to stand on the proper ground was right but that they also should maintain spiritual fellowship with all those who stand on the same ground. Suppose the brothers in Pingtung say, "We will not have any contact with you who are in Taipei. It is good enough that we have the proper ground in Pingtung." Locally, they are correct, but universally, they are divisive. Hence, we have to help people see that while the ground is local, fellowship is universal.

The Seriousness of the Ground of the Church

Someone else once asked, "If the Holy Spirit does not have the authority in the church, will God raise up another church?" The book of Revelation shows us that the ground of the church is a very serious matter. It is so serious that even though some of the seven churches in Revelation were in a state of confusion—even having idols and fornication—the Lord did not ask the believers to leave those churches. The proper ground is a serious thing. For example, we cannot say that we no longer want to be Chinese because our country is not good. We cannot do this because the ground of China has already been given to us. It is the same with the ground of the church and with any other ground. If my son comes to me one day and tells me that he is no longer my son because he has become a bandit, I would have to say that although he is a bandit, he is still my son. If he is as good as the Lord Jesus, he is my son, and if he is so bad that he becomes a bandit, he is still my son. Very few people are clear about the ground of the church to such an extent.

The Reason for Not Being United with Christian Organizations

Undoubtedly, today's Christianity has lost the ground of the church. Moreover, we can say that there are, in fact, very few people who know the ground of the church. Furthermore, today's Christianity is also full of confusion. These are the reasons why we cannot cooperate with Christianity. The first reason, of course, is a matter of the ground. We cannot cooperate with Christianity because we have a different ground. The second reason is that Christianity is full of confusion—there is great confusion in their teachings concerning the church. The third reason is that we want to show God's children a pure way. The fourth reason is that Christianity has its own mission and we have our ministry. What God has committed to us, we will do. What God has not committed to us, we will not do. We hope that we will be faithful to what the Lord has committed to us. If we cannot fulfill the commission we have received, how can we help others do their work? In the early days when we first preached the truth concerning salvation through faith, we suffered much criticism. Some pastors said, "We have been pastors for our whole life, but we are still not clear as to whether or not we are saved. How can you say that you are saved once you believe?" One time I was preaching the gospel in Suchow Gospel Hospital. I said that once we believe in the Lord, we are saved. That day my preaching was based on John 3:16: "For God so loved the world that He gave His only begotten Son, that every one who believes into Him would not perish, but would have eternal life." Incredibly, an old pastor in the audience was shaking his head. Nevertheless, after we fought the battle for this truth, all the churches in China began to preach salvation by faith. Now we are not the only ones who preach salvation by faith, but wherever we go, we can hear such preaching.

Many years ago all the believers in Christianity in China addressed one another as fellow "church friends." But since the Lord has raised us up, we have truly experienced that we are those who have the Lord's life. Furthermore, the Bible does not say that the believers are fellow church members but that they are fellow citizens with the saints and members of the household of God (Eph. 2:19). Therefore, we began to address one another as "brother" or "sister." This was also opposed by Christianity. However, today nearly no one uses the term "church friend." Formerly, it was also rare to hear terms such as "edification meeting," "fellowship meeting," "gospel meeting," "prayer meeting," and "bread-breaking meeting." Rather, all we heard was "big worship," "small worship," or "family worship." Now, however, many people in the denominations also use the word "meeting." In the past, they used the expression "taking Holy Communion" instead of "breaking bread," but now many of them also say "breaking bread." When we were first raised up by the Lord, we were not welcomed. The critical matter, however, is whether or not we have the proper ground and whether or not we are contending for the right thing. If we are contending for the right thing and standing on the proper ground, then one day those who oppose us and those who do not like us will have to take our way and do what we do. If we had not fought in the early days, there would not be any hope for the church. Therefore, we should not judge anything before its time. We have to know what we have been committed with and what we are doing.

Everyone loves to say, "We are almost the same." But we do not like to say this because many things are in fact very different. Are we really almost the same as the denominations? If we are almost the same as the denominations, we do not need to have the proper ground. From the very first day we started to take the way of the church, we declared that the whole of Christianity in China had already lost the matter of the ground. By God's mercy, we have picked up the matter of the ground. Because we picked up the ground of the church, many also became clear about this matter and therefore returned to the ground of the church. Today those in Christianity cannot but confess that we who are standing on this ground are the church. However, they wish that we would call their meeting the church as well. This is really a difficult situation. Since they call themselves the Baptist Church, the Presbyterian Church, and the Episcopalian Church, how can we call their meetings the church? They are denominations because they have lost the ground of the church. It is because they have forsaken this ground that we, by the Lord's mercy, have picked it up.

We all have to confess that the church is one. In the church in Corinth, some said that they were of Paul, of Apollos, of Peter, or of Christ. At the end, they all were rebuked by the Holy Spirit. If today some say, "I am of the Presbyterian Church" or "I am of the Baptist Church," do you think that God will approve of this? Certainly not. If God does not approve of this, should we still take newly saved ones to the Baptist Church or the Presbyterian Church? May God show us that we are compelled by necessity to start a new meeting outside of the Christian organizations such as the Presbyterian Church and the Baptist Church. Since we cannot belong to the Presbyterian Church or to the Baptist Church, we surely have to meet together by ourselves.

It is very clear who should bear the responsibility of division. On the one hand, Christianity has spread the gospel, but on the other hand, Christianity has also divided the church.

ABOUT THE AUTHOR

Witness Lee was born in 1905 in northern China and raised in a Christian family. At age 19 he was fully captured for Christ and immediately consecrated himself to preach the gospel for the rest of his life. Early in his service, he met Watchman Nee, a renowned preacher, teacher, and writer. Witness Lee labored together with Watchman Nee under his direction. In 1934 Watchman Nee entrusted Witness Lee with the responsibility for his publication operation, called the Shanghai Gospel Bookroom.

Prior to the Communist takeover in 1949, Witness Lee was sent by Watchman Nee and his other co-workers to Taiwan to ensure that the things delivered to them by the Lord would not be lost. Watchman Nee instructed Witness Lee to continue the former's publishing operation abroad as the Taiwan Gospel Bookroom, which has been publicly recognized as the publisher of Watchman Nee's works outside China. Witness Lee's work in Taiwan manifested the Lord's abundant blessing. From a mere 350 believers, newly fled from the mainland, the churches in Taiwan grew to 20,000 in five years.

In 1962 Witness Lee felt led of the Lord to come to the United States, settling in California. During his 35 years of service in the U.S., he ministered in weekly meetings and weekend conferences, delivering several thousand spoken messages. Much of his speaking has since been published as over 400 titles. Many of these have been translated into over fourteen languages. He gave his last public conference in February 1997 at the age of 91.

He leaves behind a prolific presentation of the truth in the Bible. His major work, *Life-study of the Bible,* comprises over 25,000 pages of commentary on every book of the Bible from the perspective of the believers' enjoyment and experience of God's divine life in Christ through the Holy Spirit. Witness Lee was the chief editor of a new translation of the New Testament into Chinese called the Recovery Version and directed the translation of the same into English. The Recovery Version also appears in a number of other languages. He provided an extensive body of footnotes, outlines, and spiritual cross references. A radio broadcast of his messages can be heard on Christian radio stations in the United States. In 1965 Witness Lee founded Living Stream Ministry, a non-profit corporation, located in Anaheim, California, which officially presents his and Watchman Nee's ministry.

Witness Lee's ministry emphasizes the experience of Christ as life and the practical oneness of the believers as the Body of Christ. Stressing the importance of attending to both these matters, he led the churches under his care to grow in Christian life and function. He was unbending in his conviction that God's goal is not narrow sectarianism but the Body of Christ. In time, believers began to meet simply as the church in their localities in response to this conviction. In recent years a number of new churches have been raised up in Russia and in many eastern European countries.

OTHER BOOKS PUBLISHED BY
Living Stream Ministry

Titles by Witness Lee:

Abraham—Called by God	0-7363-0359-6
The Experience of Life	0-87083-417-7
The Knowledge of Life	0-87083-419-3
The Tree of Life	0-87083-300-6
The Economy of God	0-87083-415-0
The Divine Economy	0-87083-268-9
God's New Testament Economy	0-87083-199-2
The World Situation and God's Move	0-87083-092-9
Christ vs. Religion	0-87083-010-4
The All-inclusive Christ	0-87083-020-1
Gospel Outlines	0-87083-039-2
Character	0-87083-322-7
The Secret of Experiencing Christ	0-87083-227-1
The Life and Way for the Practice of the Church Life	0-87083-785-0
The Basic Revelation in the Holy Scriptures	0-87083-105-4
The Crucial Revelation of Life in the Scriptures	0-87083-372-3
The Spirit with Our Spirit	0-87083-798-2
Christ as the Reality	0-87083-047-3
The Central Line of the Divine Revelation	0-87083-960-8
The Full Knowledge of the Word of God	0-87083-289-1
Watchman Nee—A Seer of the Divine Revelation ...	0-87083-625-0

Titles by Watchman Nee:

How to Study the Bible	0-7363-0407-X
God's Overcomers	0-7363-0433-9
The New Covenant	0-7363-0088-0
The Spiritual Man 3 volumes	0-7363-0269-7
Authority and Submission	0-7363-0185-2
The Overcoming Life	1-57593-817-0
The Glorious Church	0-87083-745-1
The Prayer Ministry of the Church	0-87083-860-1
The Breaking of the Outer Man and the Release ...	1-57593-955-X
The Mystery of Christ	1-57593-954-1
The God of Abraham, Isaac, and Jacob	0-87083-932-2
The Song of Songs	0-87083-872-5
The Gospel of God 2 volumes	1-57593-953-3
The Normal Christian Church Life	0-87083-027-9
The Character of the Lord's Worker	1-57593-322-5
The Normal Christian Faith	0-87083-748-6
Watchman Nee's Testimony	0-87083-051-1

Available at
Christian bookstores, or contact Living Stream Ministry
2431 W. La Palma Ave. • Anaheim, CA 92801
1-800-549-5164 • www.livingstream.com